"As a student and professor of the Bible, I have come to love the study of archaeology…. *The Fisherman's Tomb* tells the story of the discovery of the tomb and bones of St. Peter under St. Peter's Basilica, combining risky excavations, oil discoveries and cataclysmic explosions in Texas, the intrigues and adventures of World War II, petty jealousy among Vatican apparatchiks, scholarly diligence and carelessness, amazing heroism — plus, above all, confirmation of the truth that Jesus made Peter the rock upon which he built his Church. What a cool book!"

— *Father Mitch Pacwa, S.J., founder and president of Ignatius Productions, EWTN host, biblical scholar, author, and speaker*

"*The Fisherman's Tomb* is a gripping archeological detective story stretching back two thousand years, a true tale of religious veneration, papal risk-taking, and scholarly feuds. It's all told in fascinating and well-documented detail by John O'Neill, who reveals a behind-the-scenes American connection to the excavations that brought Saint Peter's bones to light."

— *John Thavis,* New York Times *best-selling author of* The Vatican Diaries *and* The Vatican Prophecies

"This is one of Christianity's many great stories of faith, hope, and trust. It's drama and adventure and Providence, and John O'Neill here gives it the kind of loving treatment it deserves, one clearly born of his own dramatic encounter with faith, hope, and trust. Inspired by the witness illuminated in *The Fisherman's Tomb*, may every reader grow in these virtues, through Saint Peter's intercession."

— *Kathryn Jean Lopez, senior fellow at the National Review Institute and editor-at-large,* National Review, *coauthor of* How to Defend the Faith without Raising Your Voice

THE FISHERMAN'S
TOMB

Quo Vadis?

John O'Neill

11/18/18

THE FISHERMAN'S
TOMB

THE TRUE STORY OF THE
VATICAN'S SECRET SEARCH

JOHN O'NEILL
WITH SARAH WYNNE AND KATIE CLARK

**Our
Sunday
Visitor**

www.osv.com
Our Sunday Visitor Publishing Division
Our Sunday Visitor, Inc.
Huntington, Indiana 46750

Our Sunday Visitor Publishing Division
Our Sunday Visitor, Inc.
200 Noll Plaza
Huntington, IN 46750
1-800-348-2440

ISBN: 978-1-68192-140-2 (Inventory No. T1863)
eISBN: 978-1-68192-141-9
LCCN: 2017964399

Cover design: Lindsey Riesen
Cover art: Shutterstock

PRINTED IN THE UNITED STATES OF AMERICA

About the Author

John O'Neill is a lawyer and a #1 *New York Times* best-selling author. He has spent much of his life visiting and researching early Christian sites. He is a 1967 graduate of the Naval Academy, a former law clerk to Supreme Court Chief Justice William Rehnquist, and senior partner at a large international law firm.

Dedication

To Diane O'Neill, without whom I could never have written this book, and to my brother Peter, whom I also found after long separation.

"I wonder what sort of a tale we've fallen into."

J. R. R. TOLKIEN, *The Two Towers*

CONTENTS

Foreword *15*

Chapter One
The Visit *19*

Chapter Two
George Strake *27*

Chapter Three
Peter *37*

Chapter Four
The Great Fire of Rome *41*

Chapter Five
Vatican Hill *45*

Chapter Six
Pius's Gamble *55*

Chapter Seven
Pope Pius XII and His Team *59*

Chapter Eight
The Clues in the Vatican Library *67*

Chapter Nine
Into the City of the Dead *73*

Chapter Ten
Inside the Tomb *79*

Chapter Eleven
The Three Amigos *87*

Chapter Twelve
The War *91*

Chapter Thirteen
The Flood and the Curse *103*

Chapter Fourteen
Margherita Guarducci *111*

Chapter Fifteen
The Inscriptions Speak *123*

Chapter Sixteen
The Bones Speak *129*

Chapter Seventeen
Ferrua's Revenge *133*

Chapter Eighteen
The Necropolis Uncovered *139*

Chapter Nineteen
Guarducci Alone: A New Beginning *145*

Chapter Twenty
Return of the Apostle *155*

Chapter Twenty-One
The Great Persecution and Helena *159*

Afterword *165*

Appendices *171*
I. The Inscriptions
II. The Conroe Oil Field
III. The Story of Vatican Hill
IV. Timeline
V. The Hottest Ticket in Rome

Notes and Acknowledgments *185*

FOREWORD

Sometimes a story finds an author rather than the reverse. After writing the #1 *New York Times* Best Seller, *Unfit for Command*, in 2004, I resolved not to write again, despite numerous offers, requests, and even suggested stories.

I came to Houston in 1975 after graduating from the Naval Academy and the University of Texas School of Law, followed by a clerkship at the United States Supreme Court. For years I was deeply involved as a lawyer in representing many oil companies and pipelines, and sometimes suing them. From this I knew, of course, the near legendary stories circulating in the oil industry of the great George Strake and his unlikely discovery of the immense Conroe field near my home in Houston. I only learned the story of this secretive man, however, when his son and grandchildren became my friends. Through them and much independent research, I came to know of his largely undisclosed but immense financial support of the Catholic Church and, in particular, the special projects of Popes Pius XII and Paul VI, including the search for the grave of the Apostle Peter.

Since early childhood, I have been a student of Roman and early Christian history and archeology. My love of these subjects and a restless soul have taken me to many major archeological sites, from Christian catacombs south of Istanbul, to Crete and sites in North Africa. When I began to look into the search for Peter's grave, financed by George Strake, I immediately ran into the amazing story of the great pioneer woman, archeologist Margherita Guarducci, and her epic battle over many years with a Vatican priest and archeologist, Father Antonio Ferrua. I have spent a lifetime researching massive international legal cases involving subjects as diverse as a 1988 oilfield case with the People's Republic of China and cases in places like Colombia, Ecuador, and Kazakhstan. Because of those experiences, I was able to track the numerous technical works written in Italian, Spanish, German, and even Latin and Greek, tied to the search for Saint Peter's tomb.

Stemming from this background, I felt compelled to write a book telling the great, true story of the seventy-five-year search for Peter's grave. It was only the serendipitous coincidence of my home in Houston, friendship with the Strakes, familiarity with oil exploration, love of and familiarity with Roman and Christian archeology, and a lifetime of research in complex international matters that made it possible to gather and record (with the assistance of many others, including my coauthors) the facts of this extraordinary story. I felt that, after seventy-five years, this was a story the world needed to hear.

Understanding both the facts of this story and the need to record it, I nonetheless dithered, doing little writing. Several years ago, I was suddenly diagnosed with four distinct types of cancer — throat, head, back, and legs. In the course of treatment, I contracted the dreaded MRSA bacterial infection. My chances of survival were less than 5 percent. I was and am not afraid of dying, having stared death in the face many times in Vietnam and elsewhere. However, I was afraid of dying with this story untold.

My prayer and my promise was that I would survive at least long enough to record the facts of this great story — that it would not die unrecorded with me. I thank my great coauthors, my wonderful friend and agent, Jeff Carneal, and many others who made this book possible. Most of all, I thank God for the time and breath to write it.

A slaughter and persecution of ancient Christian communities in the Middle East is underway today, even using the familiar, dehumanizing tools of crucifixion, fire, and rape employed by the persecutors of Christians in the ancient Roman Empire. These Christians are the true brothers and sisters in faith of the brave Christians depicted in this book. Inspired by George Strake, I contribute all proceeds I receive from this book to their relief.

— John O'Neill

CHAPTER ONE

THE VISIT

Today

It's arguably one of the best-kept secrets in Rome, Italy. Reservations for the tour are hard to obtain, as tours are limited to about 250 people per day. *Travel+Style* magazine calls it "one of Rome's hottest tickets,"[1] and the *Boston Globe* warns that it's "one of the toughest tickets to come by in the Eternal City."[2] The exclusive tour of the newly opened necropolis beneath St. Peter's Basilica, called the Scavi Tour,[3] takes visitors on a fascinating journey through one of Rome's oldest mysteries — but the tour only tells part of the story. The mystery itself goes back nearly two thousand years, and the Vatican's top-secret search for answers lasted for decades, involving some of the brightest minds and one of the wealthiest men of the twentieth century.

Spring 1940

The priest came to Houston likely early in 1940. He was an emissary sent directly from Rome by Pope Pius XII. The world was in flames with the onset of World War II, and monsters like Hitler, Stalin, and Tojo stalked the globe almost unhindered. Poland had been conquered in three weeks by Nazi Panzers, aided by Soviet armies. The Japanese

Empire held large parts of China and looked hungrily south to the oilfields of Indonesia. Blackshirts in Italy marched daily outside the Vatican, inspired by the buffoon Mussolini and dreams of repeating ancient Roman glory. German Panzers gathered on the Western Front soon to crush France in a new type of war called the Blitzkrieg. America slept amidst the chaos of war.

The priest's name was Walter Carroll. Although only thirty years old, Carroll was among the most trusted confidants of the pope. He was the right hand of the pope's right hand man, Papal Secretary Giovanni Montini, better known now as Pope Paul VI.[4] Father Carroll would die young — before the age of forty — but in that short time he would have a huge impact on the world, both during and after the war. As he stepped off the plane in Houston, Texas, however, he confronted a mission far more important and more lasting than the war.[5]

Texas was an unusual destination for a papal emissary on an urgent mission. He had come to see a Texas oilman and wealthy Catholic named George Strake. Strake was among the largest single donors in the world to Catholic projects, and he requested that all his donations be made anonymously. Because this meeting took place in secret, the details have been lost to history. The meeting likely took place at the Strake home, which still stands at 3214 Inwood Drive in Houston's River Oaks Subdivision. The then newly constructed English home on an acre backing up to Houston's most prestigious country club was among the largest and most stylish in the city. Houston, then a city of 400,000, had largely avoided the Great Depression due to the vast oil reserves surrounding it, its great port, and the ingenuity of its businessmen.

No record remains, except perhaps in Vatican archives, of the precise words of that meeting. However, it became a part of the heritage of the Strake family. Carroll came to Strake with a highly sensitive request from Pope Pius XII and Monsignor Montini: the Catholic Church sought Strake's commitment to finance a special project. Carroll explained that this project, one of the most important in the Church, would involve immense, uncertain cost. Moreover, if Strake agreed to finance it, he could tell absolutely no one about it. In effect, the Church was asking Strake to sign a blank check, without credit or reward, for a totally secret, wildcat project of very doubtful success.

Strake thought about the strange request and agreed.

February 11–14, 1939

The secret project that sent Carroll to Strake had begun to unfold in Rome a few months earlier, also in a very unlikely place. Pope Pius XI died on February 11, 1939. The deceased pope was an extraordinary man, mentor and spiritual father to many, both rich and poor, and well loved by many, particularly by Eugenio Pacelli, his successor. As a serious mountain climber, Pius XI was the first to summit several peaks in the Alps which are now named for him.[6] A Chilean glacier, the Pio XI, the largest in South America,[7] also bears his name.[8] Before he became pope, Pius XI (then Ambrogio Damiano Achille Ratti) had been the Vatican librarian — the keeper of the Vatican's secrets. He was plucked from the Vatican Library and, against his wishes, turned into a papal diplomat. He was known for his no-nonsense attitude, unusual in an age of formalism and ceremony. Before he died, Pius XI asked only to be buried under St. Peter's Basilica in a simple grave.

In the middle of February 1939, an excavation team began to dig beneath the basilica for both a grave for the deceased pope and a small chapel to surround it.[9] Because the area below the Vatican was only six feet high and the floor of the immense structure loomed above, they had to dig down. In the process, a workman fell through the floor. Very quickly he found himself in an amazing and until-then unknown world, with bright mural paintings of flowers (particularly roses), birds, vases full of vividly colored fruit, idyllic landscapes, cupids, and pretty winged beings.[10] The dark and gloomy underworld starkly contrasted with the bright rainbow of colors in the paintings. Vatican officials rapidly determined that the paintings were Roman funeral murals from the height of Rome's power during the first and second centuries. Digging further, the workmen discovered the remains of the daughter of a Roman consul, wrapped in purple garb with a golden brooch. Then they encountered the most amazing find of all: the much simpler grave of a woman from the mid-second century, with Christian inscriptions on her tomb.[11]

This was an astounding discovery. During its first few centuries, Christianity was a secret, illegal cult in the Roman Empire, and Christians were subject to terrible waves of persecution. Few, if any, Christian artifacts survived from this early period.[12] Across the entire Mediterranean world, Christian inscriptions or signs from the first and second centuries are extraordinarily rare.[13] To date, archeologists have uncovered a few inscriptions in a hidden cave south of Istanbul, various marks in the catacombs, coded messages through the fish symbol (the ichthus), the Good Shepherd, the altered cross, and the like. The workers and Vatican officials were stunned at the discovery of this early Christian woman's grave.

Blood sport was a popular form of entertainment in the Roman Empire. During waves of persecution Christians were captured, tortured, and publicly killed before large, enthusiastic crowds. Sometimes they were crucified, burned, boiled, or torn to pieces by wild animals in front of appreciative and wildly cheering spectators. At best, the remainder of the Christians' families would be enslaved and their property seized. Informers were incentivized by a share of the victim's property. Sometimes captured Christians were tortured until they gave up the names of other believers. The Roman governor Pliny, writing to Emperor Trajan, noted his frustration that many Christians even under torture would not recant. One such brave Christian, a young mother named Perpetua, was stripped of her baby and sent to be torn apart by wild beasts in A.D. 203. She would not recant even to stay with her baby. The Christians were incomprehensible to Roman authorities, but they saw them as superstitious enemies whose elimination was required by the *dignitas* of Imperial Rome.[14]

In those days, the Roman Empire stretched from Persia in the east to Land's End in England in the west, and from Melk in Austria and German outposts to the deep North African desert. The Empire had seldom lost a war in its long history, and even its battlefield losses were few. It achieved a degree of engineering, wealth, and civilization that would not again be reached for many centuries. The famous Pax Romana had descended on the Mediterranean world.

The impudence of the small Christian cult in honoring as God a criminal condemned by Roman law was intolerable to Rome, if also regarded as somewhat insane. Indeed, the world must have (not illogically) perceived the failure of the small cult to disband as crazy. Christians were

viewed as a particularly secretive cult, accused of practic-
ing horrific rituals. They were unpopular and risked death
if discovered. As a result, they could not leave any traceable
public display of their beliefs. They were a cult of caves and
catacombs. Thus, the 1939 discovery of Christian inscriptions deep in the seat of Roman power — a few hundred
yards from the place where the Emperor's palace once
stood — was hardly believable.[15] All work ceased, and the
highest Vatican official was summoned to verify with his
own eyes this improbable find.

Papal Secretary of State Eugenio Pacelli, soon to be
elected as Pope Pius XII, was responsible for burying his predecessor. This discovery of an early Christian's grave under
the Vatican reminded him of an ancient Christian legend.
Christian tradition from earliest times held that the Apostle
Peter had gone to Rome and, after his nearby execution by
the Emperor Nero around A.D. 66, had been buried on Vatican Hill.[16] A number of first- and second-century writings
supported this tradition, ranging from Tacitus's description
of Nero's slaughter of Christians following the Great Fire
of Rome to early second-century Christian accounts.[17] The
tradition further related that 250 years after Peter's death,
Emperor Constantine had built the first St. Peter's Basilica
in Rome as a memorial to Peter directly over his grave.[18]
Secret excavations by the Church in 1513 and 1683 to verify
the truth of the long-standing tradition found only pagan
graves, however, and the Church abandoned any further effort to find Peter. While the burial place of Peter is a pious
tradition and not a matter of faith, the Church — facing
the pressures across Europe, especially in the onslaught of
the Protestant Reformation — feared unnecessarily rattling
the dearly held beliefs of the Catholic faithful.[19] Very likely,
discovering a foundation of pagan graves, rather than the

tombs of saints, under the Church's principal and historical seat of authority would have added fuel to the fires of controversy that already raged around Rome in the sixteenth and seventeenth centuries. As later described by Margherita Guarducci, the famous archeologist who would become the heroine of the Vatican excavations: "The fear of finding something down there which would contradict or modify the tradition dear to the faithful overcame the desire to appease a burning curiosity."[20]

Since his earliest childhood, Pope Pius XII (who grew up in Rome) had been consumed by stories of the early Roman martyrs. He also believed deeply in the science of archeology. Faced with the discovery of a Christian tomb beneath the Vatican, he decided to recommence the Church's search for the first pope. Against all odds, Pius XII intended to reach across nearly two thousand years to find Peter.[21] It was a brave decision made in the face of repeated historical failure. Yet Pius XII, unlike some of his predecessors, saw science — particularly archeology — as an ally, not an enemy, of Christianity. With the increasing influence across the Western world of the work of men such as Charles Darwin, Sigmund Freud, and Karl Marx, the pope saw the immense importance of using modern science in the service of religious belief. Numerous secularists denied that the Apostle Peter ever went to Rome at all. Even Martin Luther had cast doubt upon the issue, stating, "It is unknown where in the City [of Rome] the bodies of Saint Peter and Saint Paul are located or even whether they are there at all."[22] Likely Pope Pius XII hoped that discovering the first pope's bones beneath St. Peter's Basilica would offer a tangible demonstration of the powerful interplay between faith and science. While an increasingly secular culture tried to pit the two against each other, Pius XII recognized that science and truth go hand-in-hand. Finding Peter would throw the weight of modern science behind a dearly held tradition of the Church, offering a needed boost for the faithful during a dark and often faithless time.

Yet the Church was nearly broke from the Great Depression and the Nazi occupation of Europe, so the pope first had to reach across the ocean for the immense financing necessary to carry out his plan. With his huge fortune and generosity to the Church, Texas oilman George Strake could make Pius's dream of finding Peter possible.

Strake surprisingly said yes, effectively writing a blank check to the Church. Father Carroll reported the agreement to Pius XII and Montini. Over the ensuing years, the Church privately contacted the Strakes many times about this great project. True to initial intent, both the search for Peter's remains and Strake's involvement in the search were kept wholly hidden from the world. Thus, one of the greatest explorations of the twentieth century began in the dark recesses beneath the Vatican, unknown to the outside world and cloaked in total secrecy. Over time the search would lead to the discovery of one of the greatest archeological sites of the ancient world. The adventure would involve an interesting cast of characters, including an American spy for the Vatican. After many overlooked clues and false leads, this ancient puzzle would require an unlikely woman genius and seventy-five years of searching to fully unlock. This woman's discoveries and battles would rival or exceed those of even the greatest fictional archeologists like Indiana Jones or Robert Langdon of *The Da Vinci Code*. As we shall see, truth would prove much stranger and more fantastic than fiction.

CHAPTER TWO

GEORGE STRAKE

Early Life and Career

George Strake was at birth an unlikely candidate to become one of America's wealthiest people. He was born in St. Louis, Missouri, in 1894, the youngest of ten children in an impoverished family. His parents and two of his siblings died when he was still very young, and he was raised by his two eldest sisters. The family's poverty was such that he had to drop out of school before he reached high school. He worked as a Western Union messenger boy, earning nine dollars a week. From his earliest days, he had a remarkably charitable and religious spirit. Of his nine dollars, he faithfully gave two each week to the Sunday collection at the Catholic church. The remaining seven went to his sisters for the remaining children who lived in a three-room St. Louis apartment.[23]

George was tall and gangly, endowed from the beginning with piercing blue eyes and a commanding presence that marked him as a leader. He loved reading. He was deeply inquisitive about everything and loved to learn how things worked. He didn't attend high school, but on a lark in 1913 he took the entrance exam for St. Louis University, relying only on his self-taught education. He passed the exam. When the university administrators learned he was self-taught with very little formal schooling and no money, they admitted him on a full scholarship. He was a good student who particularly enjoyed technical, financial, and engineering subjects.

He graduated in 1917, just as World War I came to America. Strake joined the Army Air Corps and became a wireless instructor and operator. After his return home, he and a wealthy young lady from Florida almost got married, but he delayed the wedding because she was rich and he was poor. She suggested he go to Mexico to find his fortune. He followed her suggestion and got a job with Gulf Oil in Tampico, Mexico. It was a wild place. Strake arrived shortly after Pancho Villa was assassinated with more than forty dum-dum bullets. The ghosts of Zapata and Madeira still haunted Mexico. War damage and carnage from the Revolution remained everywhere. Bandits were still common. In a short time, Strake rose to head of the Gulf office in Tampico, supervising nine to ten employees. He also met the woman who would become his wife, Susan Kehoe.

Strake and Susan met while both were on vacation in San Antonio. If George tended to be a bit crusty, Susan was convivial, genial, and outgoing. She never met a stranger. After they got married, it was thanks to Susan's friendly disposition that they became close friends of their neighbors in Tampico, the William Buckley family. On many occasions, they babysat the Buckleys' young children, baby Bill Buckley, Jr. (later the famous *National Review* magazine founder) and his young siblings, Jim and Pat. Their friendship led to a financial partnership. Buckley grew to love the Strakes and indicated to George that if he left Gulf Oil and went on his own, Buckley, with the assistance of some New

York banks, would finance and participate in Strake's exploration ventures.

With this assurance, Strake left the security of Gulf Oil and began pursuing oil prospects on his own as a "wildcatter." Wildcatters were the brave, slightly mad fringe of the oil industry who pursued oil discoveries in unexplored frontier areas — examples including Glenn McCarthy, portrayed in the movie *Giant*, and the legendary Columbus Marion "Dad" Joiner, who found the vast East Texas oilfield, the largest of America's oilfields in those early days. Ironically, Joiner hit oil only after selling more than 100 percent of the prospect to unsuspecting investors. Mexico was a dangerous place in the 1920s, still wildly lawless. Life was cheap there, and property rights of little regard. This was the Mexico depicted in John Huston's great movie *The Treasure of the Sierra Madre*. But unlike the prospector depicted in the film, Strake amazingly succeeded and began to turn a profit.

Strake also began investing his profits in a small U.S. startup company named Radio Corporation of America (RCA), which dealt in the new technology of "wireless" or radio. Strake knew something about this, since he had used radio in the Army Air Corps. Later, in addition to making radios, RCA started the National Broadcasting Company (NBC). Strake was successful in both his technology and oil investments. By the late 1920s, however, Strake instinctively realized the end was coming in Mexico. Strikes began at refineries and oilfields in Tampico and spread, ultimately leading to the government's seizure of the entire industry. Strake sold out and took his family out of Mexico well before the seizures, with $250,000 in profits. Grateful for his narrow escape with his wife from the increasing lawlessness and governmental expropriation there, Strake swore off Mexico.

He then turned his attention to a second industry and a new country — selling cars in Cuba. In the late 1920s Strake moved to Havana to start a car dealership (with the idea of perhaps also drilling a well or two in Cuba). After the instability of oil exploration, he wanted a stable economic foundation. In those days Ford, the dominant car manufacturer, made only black cars. Henry Ford's famous saying in the 1920s was, "Any customer can have a car painted any color that he wants so long as it is black."[24] Strake saw this as an opportunity. He believed he could sell colored cars in Cuba from other manufacturers. As it turned out, it was a very good idea at a very bad time. The Great Depression, in addition to a collapse in sugar prices, settled over Cuba, and there was little interest in buying cars of any make or color. After running through most of his fortune, Strake told Susan that they needed to get out of Cuba before they had to "swim back."

The Strakes next intended to move to Oregon to enter the more stable lumber business. Susan's mother in Houston became sick, however, and they returned there. Susan, no doubt, was pleased with this decision, as she was well loved in Houston with a wide circle of friends. Ultimately, their relocation to Houston would change their lives … and the lives of a great many other people as well.

George Strake loved to roam outdoors, using hunting or a similar excuse, while Susan nursed her mother. One area he explored near Houston lay east of the small town of Conroe, about forty miles north of Houston. During his explorations, he noticed two strange things. First, in an area southeast of the town, cattle and other livestock would not drink the brackish water. Second, in the same area, all creeks and rivers in the area of Conroe flowed northeast, moving against the southeast current of most local creeks and rivers. Thousands had gazed upon these irregularities and seen nothing, but Strake saw in them signs of a vast underground oil field. The topography and geology reminded him of the Mexican wells he had worked with near Tampico. Curious, he leased 8,500 acres at a cheap price. He took his theory and his prospect to eight different large oil companies for financing. They were not impressed, and all summarily rejected him as just another hopeless visionary peddling a sure dry hole. He had no geological staff, no exploration department, and no real track record in the United States. He had no seismic or torsion balance data. For over a decade, well after well had been drilled in the area — all without exception producing dry holes. The area was a graveyard of shattered dreams and broken companies. Strake later said the oil companies thought he was just a crazy lone wolf wildcatter, but he believed he was a "team of two" with God's help. For a long time, his proposal remained an unlikely joke to everyone except himself.

Finally, he approached Susan, told her he thought there was oil, and asked her permission to invest the very last of their money in drilling the wildcat prospect — still in the depths of the Great Depression. Although another failure like Cuba would leave them destitute, Susan agreed, expressly conditioned on thrifty George's promise to never again question anything she purchased if he hit oil.

George drilled, but hit only natural gas — a booby prize almost valueless in the early 1930s. In order to keep his leases in effect and to generate revenue for more drilling, Strake turned to a friend, W. T. Moran, a fellow Catholic (and also from the Midwest). Moran started a small refinery and filling station on the Houston-Dallas Highway to strip liquids from Strake's gas and refine and sell it as gasoline. Surviving and extending his leases on shoestring gasoline sales from one small filling station, Strake drilled a second time, with his last dollars, deeper than anyone else had drilled — nearly a mile below the earth. He hit a vast underground ocean of oil at five thousand feet deep. As it turned out, the Conroe field was an immense pool of oil sitting under a massive cap of natural gas. The geological story of its creation under the ocean over fifty-five million years ago is little short of miraculous. It was the third largest oilfield ever discovered at that time in the United States — an immense elephant field in industry slang. Strake instantly became one of the wealthiest men in the world. His brave wife, Susan, much loved in Houston, quickly became a famous shopper in Houston, New York, and Paris.

As would often happen with Strake, his discovery also made many others around him incalculably rich. As just one example, in later years, as natural gas escalated in value, Moran's right to buy the gas escalated from a single gas station into a vast fortune of utilities and pipelines, rewarding Moran many times over for his belief in Strake. A marker on the lawn of the courthouse at Conroe commemorates how Strake and his great discovery carried Conroe safely through the Great Depression and made it the "Miracle City."

On the morning of January 12, 1933, in the space of thirty seconds, George and Susan almost became poor again very quickly. Two wells operated by other companies in the Conroe Field burst into flames and then exploded with the force of a nuclear explosion. The flames could be seen many miles away. The burning wells then exploded underground and cratered, producing an immense hole swallowing up many rigs in a seemingly bottomless pit. Even after the flames were extinguished through explosives, the field continued to pour oil and gas into the six hundred-foot-deep crater, causing pressure in the remainder of the field to drop. Strake's fortune hung by a thread.

His luck held. Strake found an engineer named George Eastman who claimed to be able to stop the out-of-control holes. For the first time in oil history, Eastman drilled holes in an intentionally slanted direction (as opposed to vertical), stopping the intrusion. This technique of horizontal drilling would many years later become the basis of the fracking revolution. In 1933, against all odds, it saved the great oil field — and George Strake's immense fortune. As the world slowly tumbled toward war with the Japanese invasion of Manchuria and the Italian invasion of Ethiopia, the world price of oil increased from prices as low as $0.10 per barrel to $1.20 and more per barrel. This meant Strake's field became even more valuable, securing his position as one of the richest men in the world.

George Strake's Secret

George enjoyed a happy, fulfilling life beyond his success-ful career. He and Susan had three children, and thanks to Susan's friendly nature, they enjoyed an active and en-riching social life. She was much loved in Houston for her generous heart. The Strakes also entertained on a substan-tial scale, hobnobbing with celebrities such as Frank Sina-tra, Dorothy Lamour, Jane Russell, Robert Mitchum, and the like. George — extraordinarily thrifty himself — true to his promise, never questioned Susan's expenditures as a member of Houston society, friend to movie stars, and se-rious shopper in venues ranging from Fifth Avenue to the Via Veneto. A relative of Susan's who deeply loved her re-marked facetiously that when she died, department stores in Houston flew their flags at half-mast.

As would be expected from a veteran of World War I, a wildcatter in lawless Mexico, and a man who had worked his way from poverty to riches at least three times, George could appear stern and sometimes gruff. But unlike most other wildcatters, George had a very strange secret. He held the curious belief that he was simply a stakeholder of the vast Conroe Field, and that it was a gift from God, not the result of his own cleverness or worth. He said that far from being a crazy Lone Wolf Wildcatter, he was actually a team of two. His job was to return the field's vast wealth to the causes God approved. As a result of this conviction, he was strongly devoted to causes such as St. Joseph's Hospital, the Boy Scouts, high schools and universities, but most of all to the Catholic Church. On his desk, he kept the saying of another legendary oilman and philanthropist from Pittsburgh, Michael Benedum: "God doesn't care how much money you have when you die. God does care what you did with the money you had when you were alive."

Strake deeply feared leaving substantial funds to his children because of the corrosive effect of money. In fact, he intended to give everything away while he was still alive, even the things he loved most. In all his contributions, he demanded total anonymity. He often said that he intended to give his last dollar away anonymously with his last breath.

When Father Carroll arrived from Rome with Pope Pius XII's mysterious request for funding, he was relying on Strake's uncanny ability to see the immense possibility where others could not. Just as Strake had been able to see an unlikely underground sea of oil where no one else saw anything of value, now he saw the possibility of a monumental archeological discovery under the Vatican. Like the pope, Strake had been consumed from childhood with the early Christian Church. He was also deeply pious, reading the Bible almost every day. His faith left him in little doubt that Peter would be found. In an age when the wealthy named grand projects for themselves like Rockefeller Center or Stanford University or Carnegie Hall, Strake was insistent that nothing be named for him at all. He wanted his involvement in the Apostle Project to be kept completely secret. The pope had found the perfect participant. Strake, for his part, had found his wildest wildcat.

CHAPTER THREE

PETER

"Jesus said to them, 'Come after me, and I will make you fishers of men.' Then they abandoned their nets and followed him." — Mark 1:17–18

Who was the Apostle Peter? What were his defining characteristics? What was there that would be helpful either in identifying his mortal remains (if located) or the things associated with him? Had he really come to or remained in dangerous Rome in the age of the bloodthirsty Emperor Nero?

He was by most accounts a simple, middle class, middle-aged Jewish fisherman named Simon, of no particular note, when he met Christ near the sea of Galilee. He had been born in the village of Bethsaida in Galilee (now in Syria) around the turn of the first millennium A.D. From the Gospel account, we know his father's name was John, and he had a brother named Andrew who also became an apostle of Jesus. He was married, and Christ cured his mother-in-law of a sickness. His in-laws lived in the delightful coastal city of Capernaum. Some accounts say he had three children.

He owned his own boat on the Sea of Galilee. Peter was likely a robust and powerful man hardened by the sea and the need to throw out and pull in nets. He was all in all a typical first-century small entrepreneur without any particular import, who would have long since totally vanished from history and been forgotten but for his meeting with Christ circa A.D. 30.

Responding positively to a practical stranger's invitation to become "a fisher of men," he abandoned his home, his boat, his business, and probably his family to follow and become the leading disciple of a man whom the world would regard as an idealistic, totally impractical, quixotic dreamer. That man was called Jesus. To mark the fisherman's new work, Jesus also gave him a new name, one which was uncommon in ancient times[25] — Petros, or Peter — which means "rock." This name is given to no one else in Scripture. Although his faith often deserted him, Peter was the first to claim Jesus as the long-awaited Messiah (see Matthew 16:13). In turn, Christ gave him "the keys to the kingdom."

The road the fisherman followed from Jesus' invitation on the shore of the Sea of Galilee would have many twists and turns. He would travel far from simple Galilee over the next three decades, and would come to be venerated as the first pope, one of the greatest Christian saints, and even recognized as a great leader for the Christians by some Muslims.[26]

Was he the sort of courageous person who would actually come to and stay in Rome while he knew himself to be the target of the wrath of Nero? Or would he have fled the emperor's notorious cruelty? The answer is both. The Peter who three times denied even knowing Christ in his greatest hour of need, was the same person who sought to defend Christ against a crowd of arresting soldiers. Later, the same man who once tried and failed to walk on water would appear twice before the Sanhedrin — the same tribunal that had seized Christ — excoriating them for their cowardly and evil treatment of Jesus. Peter was clearly capable both of defying the emperor to his face on his home ground and fleeing. He was much the type of man who would first flee and then, mortified by his cowardice, return to face death.

Yet tradition holds that he stayed in Rome (or returned) and was crucified upside down around the year 65. If this ancient story proved true, what would an archeological excavation find? Most likely the relics would be those of a man in his sixties with a robust physique, bearing marks of crucifixion. The Jewish turncoat general Josephus,[27] who joined the Romans to destroy his own people, wrote of how the Roman soldiers at play would crucify Jewish captives in various different positions for their amusement. Tacitus described how Nero in particular crucified Christians upside-down. Peter's relics — if they somehow survived two thousand years — would likely show marks of violent crucifixion.

Finally, if the old legends that Christians found and preserved the remains of the first pope were actually true, surely they would have left some symbols of respect to mark the site — perhaps a cloth wrapping or hidden inscriptions (hidden, since they themselves would continue to be persecuted for 250 years after Nero). What clues might archeologists search for? Because the name "Peter" was largely unknown before Christ gave it to Simon, any discovered reference to "Petros" from the first century almost surely referred to the pope. Drawings of key symbols, particularly with a "P" or "Pe" for Petros, would be other clear ways of representing Peter.

Many secularists denied that Peter ever went to Rome. In addition, Martin Luther claimed that nobody knew where in Rome the bodies of Saints Peter and Paul were located or whether they were even there at all.[28] If the physical remnants of Peter's presence and death in Rome could be found, it would tend to validate numerous Christian and Catholic beliefs. It could provide the power of archeological and physical evidence to support early Christian writings. On the other hand, if the search failed to find evidence of Peter, it would tend to validate the skepticism of Luther and many others toward the Catholic Church and Catholic accounts of early Christian history in general.

If Peter's relics could somehow be identified, they could answer these questions across the long millennia separating his death from Pius's search. Were the descriptions of him accurate? Did he really go to Rome during the persecution of Nero? Was he crucified upside down and buried in Rome? Did his friends honor him, and how?

THE GREAT FIRE
OF ROME

(July 18–19, A.D. 64)

The monster Nero ruled the Roman Empire from A.D. 54 to 68. He is most notable to history for his unbelievable cruelty. It is rumored that he was involved in the poisoning of his adopted father (in order to become emperor) and joked about it.[29] He executed his own mother and his wife. He is said to have poisoned his brother and personally killed his pregnant second wife by kicking her to death.[30] Nero unleashed a sea of blood in the city of Rome, not sparing any class or person. He was famous for his cowardly pretensions and even awarded himself first place in an Olympic chariot-racing competition — even though he had dropped out of the race. He was a poor singer whose most notable song is said to have played while Rome burned. He was the last of the great dynasty started by Julius Caesar, a dynasty once much loved by the Roman people. Nero's reign was marked by notable military triumphs and distributions of food, treasure, and wealth to the people of Rome. But his cruelty and evil madness made him much-hated in Rome. In A.D. 68 he would be driven from power, unable to find a single

41

friend to shelter him. Ironically, he would, like Adolf Hitler in the twentieth century, exit this world with a cowardly suicide while still proclaiming his own greatness.

In the hot summer of 64, Nero planned to build the largest palace in human history in the crowded center of Rome. In addition to a large lake and gardens, he planned to construct a massive, 100-foot statute of himself, the so-called Colossus Nero, portraying him as the sun god with a rudder steering the world under his feet. To build his palace he needed land — lots and lots of land — in the densely populated center of Rome, a city of a million or more and at the time the largest city in the world.[31]

Thus the Romans and most of their contemporary historians believed it no coincidence when, on the evening of July 18, 64, a massive fire broke out in many different shops southeast of the Circus Maximus. It was an extraordinarily hot night, even for Rome, with high winds blowing. The fire rushed up Rome's fashionable Palatine Hill, destroying the most ancient parts of the city. The ancient temple of Rome's patron god, Jupiter, burned, along with the Forum. The fire also reached the Subura District crowded with wooden, multistory apartment houses. The fire burned for six days and seven nights — in the end damaging or completely destroying ten of the fourteen districts of Rome.[32]

Reports of fires set by systematic arsonists swept through Rome. Nero claimed much of the destroyed area for his grand palace, leading Romans to suspect that Bloody Nero himself, despite his hypocritical protestations of concern for the victims, had set the Great Fire.[33] To save face, Nero (like Hitler centuries later) settled upon a small, unpopular cult to blame for the fire.[34] The Christians, who worshipped as God an alleged criminal executed by the Romans, were a perfect target. Nero unleashed upon the

Christians an incredibly cruel persecution, even by ancient standards.[35]

The place of their torture and execution was Nero's gardens and circus, built in anticipation of the grand palace, known as the Domus Aurea — the Golden House.[36] He had the Christians (men and women) dipped in oil and then wrapped in flammable cloth and materials, hoisting them in the air on posts and burning them alive as human candles to light his gardens. He sewed women and children into animal skins and released dogs to tear them apart. He crucified Christians by the hundreds, sometimes upside down. Even hardened Romans like the historian Tacitus found his treatment of the Christians extraordinarily cruel.[37] His cruelty apparently did not offend the large, cheering Roman crowds.

Christian tradition and later writings relate that during this persecution Nero located, condemned, and executed the two great leaders of the early Christian Church — Peter and Paul.[38] These traditions hold that Peter, after long, horrible imprisonment, was crucified upside down, at his request.[39] He did not consider himself worthy to die as Jesus had. Tradition further relates that the Roman executioners discarded Peter's body on the ground on a nearby, vacant hill used as a dumping ground for waste, but that Christians secretly recovered and buried Peter's body on that hill.[40] The traditions claimed the site became almost immediately a secret place of worship for the Christians. The name of that place was Vatican Hill.

CHAPTER FIVE

VATICAN HILL

Today Vatican City, measuring 110 acres, is the seat of the Catholic Church, home of the pope, and the smallest sovereign state in the world. More than half of it consists of gardens, some dating back to A.D. 1200. In addition to St. Peter's Square and the Renaissance-era St. Peter's Basilica, Vatican City contains perhaps the greatest collection of historical art and statuary in the world. In the Vatican Museum, the history of the West is contained in ancient statues like the Three Graces weaving, nurturing, and finally cutting the Thread of Life. The full-size statue of Caesar Augustus (Prima Porta Augustus) stares down as if frozen in the first century, while Madonnas by Titian and Raphael are mixed with Da Vinci's *St. Jerome in the Wilderness*, leading to Michelangelo's great ceiling in the Sistine Chapel.

Immediately outside the Sistine Chapel, Michelangelo executed his last great fresco, *The Crucifixion of St. Peter*. The image depicts Peter crucified upside down on Vatican Hill. Michelangelo even depicted himself as a sad bystander, observing Peter's death. Little did he know that his painting would become both a clue and a confirmation in the search for Peter centuries later.

A gallery of more than three thousand stone tablets and inscriptions describes history, along with the funeral sarcophagus of Roman Empress Helena of the West (who also played a part in the story of the search for Peter). But amazingly and totally unknown to the world until the Apostle Project, the greatest historical gallery of the Vatican was not in the Vatican but *under* it, where the history of an age lay silent, frozen, and inviolate for almost two thousand years.

To understand the complexity of the Apostle Project undertaken by Pius XII, one must travel back almost two millennia. In fact, Vatican Hill has a complex history and structure. The hill that now boasts the enormous St. Peter's Basilica was once a worthless, sandy hill located outside the walls of Rome. Unusable for farming, for uncounted centuries it had been used as a dumping ground for bodies of slaves, animals, and the poor. It lay west of the Tiber River and the heart of Rome. Caligula built a racetrack near the hill during his reign, and nearby were the gardens where Nero would inflict his cruelty.

Within a short time after Peter's death, Christians began to worship secretly at a spot on Vatican Hill where they believed Peter had been buried.[41] Through waves of persecution as the years went on, Christians would climb the hill to the place where they believed Peter had been buried. But the hill did not long remain vacant. Prominent pagan families began to use the area as a burial ground, and the hill gradually became a necropolis of 250 years' worth of mostly pagan graves.

The worst of the persecutions of Christians — under the emperors Valerian and Diocletian — occurred around 250 to 313, after which the storm lifted. The persecutions largely came to an end when the Roman Emperor Constantine (c. 300–337) rose to power.[42] After his 312 victory at Milvian Bridge, where he claimed to see a cross in the sky with the words, "In this sign you shall conquer,"[43] he took control of the western Roman Empire and, together with the emperor of the East, published the Edict of Milan, thus granting Christians the freedom to worship.[44] Later, when he gained control of the whole Roman Empire, Constantine moved the capital from Rome to Constantinople. He apparently remained a pagan for most or all of his life, but he acceded to the requests of his Christian mother, Helena, and allowed a church to be built over the site traditionally held to be Peter's grave near the top of Vatican Hill.[45]

The planned church needed a level foundation, and Vatican Hill was anything but flat. Peter's purported grave stood near, but not at the top, surrounded by the family tombs of numerous prominent families. Desecration of these burial sites would generate widespread hatred of the emperor. The Romans — perhaps history's greatest engineers — solved the problem by filling the hill with millions of feet of fill around the numerous existing pagan tombs.[46] The effect was to create a vast, hidden, underground necropolis, which would remain frozen in time and space under the new church.

Roman Family Tombs

The supreme memorial to a Roman family's dignity and history was its family tomb, containing the ashes, busts, and portraits of generations of family members, many going back hundreds of years. In Rome, the basic social unit was the family. The *pater familias* — the senior male — had the power of life and death over all family members and was in turn himself responsible to the Republic for their actions. Much of the standing and *dignitas* of a citizen was his family's standing. The family tomb thus became, in effect, a museum of family history (and with it the history of Rome), designed to celebrate ancestors while impressing passers-by with the family's *gravitas*. The most well-known entrance to Rome — the Appian Way — was lined on either side by many of the family tombs of the great families of Roman history, such as the Julia, Scipii, Horatia, Cornelii, and Graccii families.[47] It is no accident that the poet Thomas Babington Macaulay portrays the legendary Roman hero Horatius, facing certain death defending a bridge in Rome, proclaiming:

> To every man upon this earth
> > Death cometh soon or late.
> And how can man die better
> > Than facing fearful odds
> For the ashes of his fathers
> > And the temples of his gods?[48]

Centuries of looting began with the Visigoths' conquest and sack of Rome in 410, followed by the Vandals in 455, the Saracens in 846, and the Germans in 1527. The great family tombs of the Appian Way were reduced to ruins.[49] With the barbarian invasions, the Empire died. Rome became a city of ancient ruins, the Colosseum half collapsed, the Forum and Senate House mere rubble, and famous baths and homes now merely stones and fading memories. But the family tombs under the Vatican had a different fate. As civilization in the West died to a flicker with the great barbarian invasions of the Roman Empire, even the memory of the legendary surviving family tombs inadvertently preserved by Constantine under the Vatican disappeared. Because of Constantine's engineering, they (unlike the tombs on the Appian Way) survived the great invasions of Rome. Unknown to the invaders, they remained wholly intact as they had been in 337 when they were buried beneath the newly constructed basilica. The outside world knew only of a few legends and ancient writings in the Vatican archives about Peter's grave. The rest of the tombs beneath the basilica were left suspended in time and space.

Outside, the world changed. The capital of the Empire was moved to Constantinople, where it would exist for one thousand years until the Turkish conquest in 1453. Eventually the capital of the Western Empire would move again, this time to Ravenna. Rome moved from the center of the Roman world to its periphery. In the late fourth century, the Roman legions, once the dominant military force of the world, were shattered — first by war between themselves. Then waves of invaders, like wolves sensing the weakness of their prey, brought the Empire in the West to an end. The Visigoths under Alaric shattered the Roman armies while looting Rome. They were followed by the Vandals, whose name survives as a description of their habit of pointless destruction. Because of faith or superstition, these hordes did not destroy the wooded St. Peter's Basilica itself, although the Vandals certainly stripped and looted it. But with the death of all involved in the construction of the church, the destruction of the great families of Rome, and the eradication of almost all written records relating to St. Peter's (as well as almost all those who could read them), the waves of destruction passed through Rome and the West leaving the forgotten tombs buried underneath St. Peter's unknown and untouched.

When literacy and learning began to return to the West, there were no records left to tell the popes or Michelangelo, Raphael, the Medici, or Bernini that a few yards beneath their feet lay one of the greatest surviving storehouses of Roman art and history in the world. Ironically, the tombs hidden below the feet of the famed Renaissance painters and sculptors held early versions, some 1,500 years old, of many of the same themes embraced by Titian, Botticelli, Rubens, and many great painters. Leda met the Swan and beautiful Venus reclined in the dark-filled tombs unknown to the world.

The New Basilica

St. Peter's Basilica, as constructed, was built of wood and measured over 340 feet in length. It was completed around 337 and became the focal point of Christianity for 1,200 years. In the wooden church, much of the history of the West occurred. It housed events such as the crowning of Charlemagne as Emperor of the West in 800. Numerous kings and emperors were enthroned and buried there. More than two hundred popes over one thousand years were elected and then enthroned within its walls. They ranged from saints and heroes to the Borgia popes indifferent to the spiritual. But the long parade of popes and history did not disturb the ancient tombs underneath the basilica. The tombs continued their long sleep, unknown to the world. Although for most of its life located outside Rome's walls, defenseless and made of wood, the old basilica, while often looted, was amazingly never burned or destroyed.

Around 1450, it became apparent that the one-thousand-year-old wooden church was beginning to collapse. Popes Nicholas V and Julius II were determined to replace the old St. Peter's with a new, immense basilica. Old St. Peter's had survived the Vandals and the Saracens, but it did not survive the grand reconstruction plans. The historic St. Peter's was almost totally destroyed, mindlessly obliterating wonderful artwork, sculpture, and crypts, many dating back one thousand years.

Among the destroyed works of art were frescoes and mosaics created by Giotto and other masters of the late

Middle Ages. Tragically, these works survive now only in ancient accounts and scattered fragments. The tombs of more than one hundred popes were eradicated, along with other burial sites and memorials. In fact, the destruction wrought by the construction vastly exceeded that caused by time and even the waves of looters. Thankfully, the builders did leave intact the old altar and foundations, simply building over them. Beneath it all, the Necropolis continued its thousand-year sleep, remaining unknown and untouched through the construction of the immense new church.

Pope Julius II, the moving force behind the new St. Peter's, intended to have a vast tomb for himself on the main floor of the new basilica. The tomb was to be constructed by Michelangelo. Although Michelangelo constructed a much reduced model of the vast tomb Julius intended, it was placed in a different church after Julius's death, and Julius never rested there. Instead, in an illustration of the vagaries of politics, pomp, and power, the immensely powerful Julius was buried without a monument of any kind in the floor of the Vatican. Today he is remembered only by a simple and difficult to locate marble slab.

In 1626, an excavation to install Bernini's bronze baldacchino[50] deeply encroached into the Necropolis.[51] The excavation revealed various pagan tombs including a sarcophagus of one Flavius Agricola.[52] Flavius, whose image reclined full length with a wine cup on the lid, advised through an inscription:

> Mix the wine, drink deep, wreathed in flowers, and do not refuse to pleasure pretty girls. When death comes, earth and fire devour all.[53]

The priests and workmen, horrified by the discovery of a pagan libertine rather than a saint beneath the basilica's

main altar, immediately dumped portions of the sarcophagus into the Tiber, sealed the site, and kept the inscription
secret in the Vatican Library. This was, after all, the notorious era of the "fig leaf campaign," when nude portions of
Michelangelo's *The Last Judgment* were painted over or covered and fig leaves painted over ancient Roman statutes in
the Vatican.

Periodic later excavations likewise found pagan
graves rather than saints, suggesting the horrifying possibility that the great seat of Christianity rested not on the tomb
of saints, but on the graves of pagans. As mentioned earlier,
Protestant leaders such as Luther questioned whether Peter
had ever come to Rome at all.[54] They denounced as frauds
the great basilica and the papacy itself, which claimed to be
descended from Peter.

In 1939, the long sleep of two millennia was about to
end. In February of that year, at his specific request, Pope
Pius XI was buried in grottos under the altar of St. Peter's,
alongside Emperor Otto II of Germany, King James III of
England,[55] Queen Christina of Sweden,[56] and many other
popes and kings. The Church determined not only to honor
his wish to be buried in the grottos, but also to surround the
grave with a chapel.

Because the grottos had low ceilings, it was decided
to lower the floor to create the chapel. Digging almost immediately uncovered beneath the floor shockingly beautiful, brightly colored, and vivid mortuary murals of cranes,
flowers, dolphins, pygmies, and even Venus rising from the
sea.[57] After first finding the elaborate tomb of a consul's
daughter, the diggers came upon the grave of a young and
clearly beloved Christian woman named Aemilia Gorgania.[58] She had been a twenty-eight-year-old wife, famous in
Rome around A.D. 150 for her beauty and innocence. She

was surrounded by Christian inscriptions including one in early Latin reading, "*Dormit in pace*" ("rests in peace")[59] together with a drawing of a woman drawing water from a well (a familiar early Christian motif for the refreshment of heaven, which also represented the story of the Samaritan woman — Christ's unlikely first messenger to a Samaritan village). Next to her were the words "sweet souled Gorgania." In a short time, other astounding discoveries of bejeweled Romans and tombs were made in the Necropolis. The work was halted and Pius XII informed of the discoveries.

Pius XII now confronted a difficult decision — namely, whether to continue to excavate under the foundations, possibly proving once and for all that Peter was not buried there, or to cease the digging as in 1626, treating the excavation as if it never happened and sealing any records in the Vatican Library. Pius XII made the incredibly brave decision to pursue the excavation. Unlike the excavators in 1626, Pius XII chose to pursue the truth. The search for the Apostle had begun, in the dark, early days of World War II. It would not end for nearly seventy-five years.

CHAPTER SIX

PIUS'S GAMBLE

The history of human institutions is a record of ephemeral lives, often with violent ends. The Golden Age of Athens, which gave birth to our greatest sculptures, as well as Socrates, Plato, and Aristotle, ended in the bloodbath of Syracuse and the Peloponnesian Wars in less than one hundred years. The long reign of Rome and the most long-lasting of Chinese and Egyptian Dynasties never reached or barely survived one thousand years. In the entire history of man, only two human institutions approach continuous existence and succession for more than two thousand years: the Japanese Imperial Succession and the papacy.

To approximately 1.2 billion human beings today, the pope is both supreme in all matters relating to the Church and infallible when, as pope, he promulgates teaching on matters involving faith and morals. Why is Rome the "headquarters" for Catholicism? On first impression, it seems an unlikely choice. Its first and most significant contact with Christianity was the criminal condemnation and crucifixion of Christ by a Roman procurator. Rome has, at best, slight biblical connections — a letter from Saint Paul to the small Roman church, an account of Paul's beheading there by Nero, and allusions to Rome as an evil Babylon.

Moreover, in Christianity's early years, Rome butchered Christians without mercy.

Ephesus, Antioch, or especially Jerusalem would seem to have a far better historical claim to be the capital of Christianity. Except for Peter. Fundamental to the legitimacy of the pope is the belief that Peter was made head of the Church by Christ, who gave him the keys to the kingdom of heaven: "And so I say to you, you are Peter, and upon this rock I will build my church, and the gates of the netherworld shall not prevail against it. I will give you the keys to the kingdom of heaven. Whatever you bind on earth shall be bound in heaven, and whatever you loose on earth shall be loosed in heaven" (Mt 16:18–19).

Catholics believe that Peter, in turn, passed on this authority to a line of successors — the popes — who succeeded to his authority, in what is known as apostolic succession. There have been 266 popes, one after another, each ruling under Peter's mandate. The first 31 popes (with only one exception) were executed by the Romans. Even despite a brief, tumultuous, sixty-eight years when the popes ruled from Avignon in France, the papal line has continued unabated, with a clear connection to Peter and to Rome.

The papacy's tie to Rome, though not foundational to the Catholic faith, has deep emotional, religious, and even political roots, and has been such an enduring part of the Church's tradition that its invalidation would be a deeply unsettling discovery. Even worse, if scientific evidence proved the long-held tradition of Peter's burial beneath the Vatican to be false, it could cause people both within and outside of the Church to call into question much more fundamental Church teachings. Pius XII, 260th in the long-claimed succession of Peter, certainly recognized this danger. If the excavations proved that Peter had never been in

Rome, the Church's credibility in other matters — especially after centuries of upheaval — might become subject to serious doubt. If Peter never really came to Rome — if he was never really the leader of a Christian community there and never really passed along his authority to a Roman successor — even the pope's authority and credibility could more easily be called into question.

Various prior and small-scale excavations by Pius's predecessors had totally failed to find Peter. Although they had been conducted in secret, the excavations in the sixteenth and seventeenth centuries had eventually become known to the public, giving critics fodder to cast some doubt on papal legitimacy. Faced with growing skepticism in the twentieth-century world, no doubt exacerbated by the chaos of worldwide war, Pius chose to take one of the great gambles in human history — excavating under the Vatican itself to prove or disprove Peter's arrival and death in Rome. Although he would seek to keep the excavations secret, he must surely have known that the results would leak out, as with the earlier efforts.

Pius's decision was a strange and wild bet for a man known to be conservative and risk-averse in most every other way. Why? Almost certainly it was no gamble at all to Pius. He had an almost irrational, unwavering faith that Peter was there and would be found. Christ told Peter (the Rock) that he would build his Church upon him. Pius firmly believed this statement to be both a symbolic truth and a literal one. He believed that Christendom's greatest church was constructed over Peter's physical remains. The immense search would prove him right — or wrong.

CHAPTER SEVEN

POPE PIUS XII AND HIS TEAM

Pius and His Dreams of Peter

If George Strake was the perfect partner for the Apostle Project, fortune or fate could not have delivered a more committed or enthusiastic leader than Eugenio Pacelli. The search for Peter in many ways began long before 1939 with the childhood dreams of Eugenio Pacelli, who took the name Pius XII when elected pope in 1939. His family was from Rome and closely connected for over a century with the Vatican. His father had been chief legal advisor to the Vatican, and Pacelli often played there as a child.

Pacelli grew up surrounded by Roman antiquities, massive architectural relics from the Roman Age like the Colosseum, the Pantheon, and the victory monuments of Roman emperors such as the Arches of Constantine and Septimus Severus, as well as even more ancient obelisks. There were ancient Christian churches throughout Rome and, of course, the Vatican itself, where his family worked. He visited the catacombs that hid the early Christians (and would later hide the Jews).

Pacelli was thin and sickly, but brilliant. He became fluent in Latin in childhood and wrote an essay about himself in 1889 at the age of thirteen, in which he stated: "I am inspired by the Classics and the study of Latin gives me the highest enjoyment."[60] He loved reading the great Latin classics — Caesar, Cicero, Virgil, and Augustine of Hippo. According to his uncle, he imagined himself an early Roman martyr, like Peter. While long years would pass from his childhood until he launched the Apostle Project,[61] Christian archeology was his lifelong passion from earliest childhood. When he gazed at the surviving ruins of the Empire throughout Rome, from monuments of glory to the humble, dark catacombs where early Christians prayed and were often caught and slaughtered, he imagined the march of the Legions and the secret gatherings of Christians.

Early Career

In 1901, at the age of twenty-five, Eugenio Pacelli was welcomed to the Vatican by a much different predecessor, Leo XIII, beginning fifty-seven continuous years of service in the Vatican that would end only with his death in 1958. Leo recognized from the beginning Pacelli's genius and used him as a pivotal diplomat for the Church. Pacelli dealt throughout his career with the totalitarian scourges of Nazism, Fascism, and Communism. From his very first year in the Vatican, when he was sent as the Vatican representative for the funeral of Queen Victoria, he was marked as the Church's greatest diplomat.

Pacelli quickly became the Vatican's go-to diplomat. In May 1917, at the age of thirty-nine, he embarked on perhaps the most important mission of his life. World War I had been the charnel house of the West, leaving many millions dead on the Western Front, in Russia, and in the strange battle of the Alps between Italy and Austria. At the request of Germany's ally, the Hapsburg Monarchy in Austria, the Church presented peace proposals to the warring powers. Pacelli met directly with German Chancellor Theobald von Bethmann-Hollweg, who reacted favorably to the peace proposals, and it appeared the Great War might end. With the collapse of Russia, however, the Kaiser decided to follow the advice of the German General Staff to launch a massive last-gasp offensive on the Western Front to break the Allies' back. He fired Bethmann-Hollweg and rejected the Vatican peace proposals. From that failure followed the hideous, totalitarian evils, which Pacelli would spend the rest of his life combatting — Fascism, Nazism, and Communism.

Pacelli remained in Germany for the next ten years, on occasion risking his life combating the Communists and the Nazis. In 1919, he witnessed a brutal massacre by the Communists in Munich and narrowly survived threats to his own life. In 1924, while still in Munich, he witnessed the failure of Hitler's Beer Hall Putsch and predicted that Hitler "was finished" and "would never be heard from again." In 1945, when the American diplomat Robert Murphy asked Pope Pius XII how his earlier prediction squared with "papal infallibility," Pius replied, "I was only a monsignor then."[62]

Pacelli played a major role in the 1929 Lateran Treaty with Mussolini, establishing the Vatican State. He was virtually a polyglot, fluently speaking at least seven languages. Despite his numerous speeches against the Nazis, he was deeply involved in the controversial 1933 Reichskonkordat between the Church and Hitler, in which the Church traded noninvolvement in the German political process for non-persecution. Critics called it a trade of silence for survival. Its only apparent alternative — confrontation of Hitler —

promised instant destruction in Germany to a Church that had already seen thousands of priests and believers executed in Mexico, Spain, and elsewhere around the globe. The future pope's participation in the negotiation of the treaty would permanently mar his reputation. The Nazis and Fascists opposed Pacelli's 1939 election to the papacy,[63] and the Nazi Security Service reported that Pacelli "had already made himself prominent by his attacks on National Socialism."[64] Pope Pius XII would soon find himself confronted not by another buffoon like Mussolini, but by Hitler, a man Pius described as "an untrustworthy scoundrel and fundamentally wicked person."[65]

In 1943, in the depth of World War II and in a Vatican literally surrounded by Nazis and Blackshirts, Pius XII issued the encyclical *Divino Afflante Spiritu* ("Inspired by the Holy Spirit"), calling for the study of early biblical texts, archeological ruins, and Jewish traditions. Calling on the Church to take a leading part in scientific research, he wrote, "It is indeed regrettable that such precious treasures of Christian antiquity are almost unknown." Pius's encyclical also noted the improvements in archeology. The encyclical did not mention the great secret archeological project he had already launched underneath the Vatican itself — the search for Peter.

In many ways, the Apostle Project required the unlikely confluence of two remarkable men whose decisions to participate would have been judged irrational, eccentric, or even insane by their contemporaries. For Pius, always described as "cautious" and diplomatic, it was clearly a case of faith and dreams overcoming lifelong risk aversion. For George Strake, it was another wildcat, and God was with him. In the most unlikely way, the moment had found the men. So too, it would in a few years find an equally unlikely, but indispensable, woman.

The Apostle Project Team

In late 1939, Pius XII organized the team he intended to use on the Apostle Project. He determined to keep the project a complete secret from the world except for the disclosure to George Strake. To ensure this secrecy, he made the fateful decision to use only priests and Vatican workers for the project. He also determined that only picks and shovels — no power tools — would be used for the work, both to avoid detection and to minimize destruction, a decision that greatly lengthened the project.[66] In effect, the excavation would be done using the same methods the Romans had used to fill the Necropolis some 1,600 years earlier. The decision to use only an inside team without outside experts would prove to be a serious mistake.

It is likely that Pius wished to prevent disillusionment of the faithful if the project once again turned up only pagan graves. Although word would almost certainly leak out eventually, he wished to control when and how the disclosure would occur. He was also probably equally concerned with any false claims of success. Finally, the Fascists, who held power throughout Italy, were obsessed with their Roman heritage, even destroying the great Capitoline Hill to build the pseudo-Roman Victor Emmanuel Monument — the monstrous "wedding cake" that now stands in the center of the city. It is likely they would have interfered with and even seized control of the project had they known of it. Their very name was derived from the fasces — the bundle of rods carried by lictors in early Rome. They would clearly have gloried in the ancient Roman tombs beneath the Vatican, since they imagined themselves as the spiritual and physical descendants of the Romans.

Pius XII turned to his closest inside advisors as his team on this project.[67] He first selected Ludwig Kaas to run the excavation under the Vatican. Kaas, a German priest, had been Pius XII's closest advisor and friend during his long diplomatic efforts in pre-Nazi Germany. A longtime member of the German Reichstag and leader of the Christian Centre Party, Kaas was also deeply involved in opposition to Hitler and in support of the controversial 1933 agreement with Hitler after he had become chancellor. That support had earned him threats both from the Nazis and from those in Germany opposed to the 1933 agreement. For his safety, Kaas was moved to St. Peter's in 1935 to prevent his arrest and execution by the Nazis. It is an indication of the extreme importance of the Apostle Project that Pius selected Kaas, perhaps his closest friend in the world, as supervisor, reporting directly to the pope on its progress.

Kaas, however, had absolutely no experience in or knowledge of archeology or excavation. A priest named Antonio Ferrua, who held a 1937 doctorate in archeology, maneuvered his way onto the excavation team and soon assumed practical control of it.[68] Ferrua's actual field experience in real-world excavations was limited, as he had received his doctorate only two years before. He was a perfect bureaucratic functionary, assuming control and power through force of personality, control of access to information, and clever maneuvers. He was attentive to colleagues, wrote prolifically in journals, and assiduously courted professional associates. He had a perhaps unjustifiably high view of his own ability and bitterly resented disagreement or criticism. Involvement with the Apostle Project, as well as access to those in control, offered Ferrua a road to fame, position, and power and allowed him to demonstrate his talents. Within a short time, Ferrua had self-promoted himself into practical control of the excavation, wholly excluding Kaas from day-to-day information and treating him with contempt, only allowing him to learn of the excavation's progress through inspection or questioning individual workmen.[69] Ferrua simply refused to talk to him, causing serious problems for the project.

Ferrua was assisted by others, including a good-natured German priest from Cologne, Father Engelbert Kirschbaum, a member of the Papal Archeological Academy, of which he was the director from 1949 to 1958, and a professor of Christian Archeology who was harmonious and kind.[70] Because the team was limited to working with picks and shovels, an army of inside laborers was employed. Other Vatican officials assisted. The lighting was dim, and the site was hot, poorly ventilated, and dusty. The vast bulk of the Vatican above created a serious risk of the excavation site caving in. In the world of archeology, known for dangerous and arduous work sites, this was among the worst — hazardous, cramped, and roasting in summer.

In addition to the "inside" team, Pius XII delegated his secretary, Giovanni Montini, to form an "outside" team to deal with Strake and other critical matters. Montini was assisted by American priests Walter Carroll and later Joseph McGeough.

Unbeknownst to any of the participants as the project commenced, a young woman named Margherita Guarducci labored in Crete over long-forgotten Greek inscriptions.[71] In a male-dominated age, Church, and profession, none of the participants would have believed it possible that this unlikely woman, or any woman, would play a serious role in the Apostle Project. Eventually and ironically, she — and she alone — by force of her own genius and tenacity, would solve the great puzzle. She would make discoveries under the Vatican beyond the wildest dreams of the initial team of excavators.

Chapter Eight

The Clues in the Vatican Library

The Vatican Library houses the greatest collection of early writings in the world. With the destruction of the great Library of Alexandria and the barbarian invasions of the Roman Empire, most classical and early Christian writings were lost forever. The total cultural history of Greece, Rome, and the West nearly perished in the ashes of the Empire. Numerous plays by Sophocles, writings by the great Greek philosophers, detailed Roman histories, and early Christian writings were completely destroyed. The entire heritage of the West might itself have become like Egyptian and Mayan history, only a faint, dead reconstruction from faded inscriptions. But here and there ancient writings survived: at Constantinople, where the knowledge of the Old Empire was maintained until its conquest in 1453; in monasteries scattered from Ireland to Admont and Melk in Austria; at St. Peter's; and in other remote places. Over the 1,600 years between construction of the old St. Peter's and 1940, the originals and copies of virtually every surviving early Christian or Roman work found their way to the Vatican Library. It housed well over a million books, manuscripts, and papyrus, as well as seventy-five thousand ancient codices, many found nowhere else in the world.

The Apostle Project team's first job before beginning the actual excavation under the Vatican was to search the ancient documents in the Vatican Library for clues and guidance to the whereabouts of Peter. Their research began in 1939–1940. Was there ancient confirmation that he really came to Rome? Was there proof that he was buried there and, if so, where and how? What markers or memorials were mentioned in ancient contemporary literature? What happened to the tomb (if it existed) in the intervening centuries of barbarian, Saracen, and German looting of the Vatican?

The Vatican Library is the ultimate repository of the Church's secrets. This is probably why the position of head librarian has always been occupied by well-regarded and very serious priests of great intelligence — such as Pius XI. The library contains works as tragic as the 1311 plea for help from 231 Knights Templar about to be burned at the stake and the final letter of Mary, Queen of Scots, awaiting execution by her relative, Queen Elizabeth I. It also contains works as trivial as Michelangelo's letters complaining over his pay for the Sistine Chapel. There is additionally an ancient "secret history" of the reign of Emperor Justinian, written about 600, and a plea from many English nobles and churchmen to the pope on behalf of Henry VIII's attempted divorce from Katharine of Aragon. The library also contains numerous documents of great historical significance, including the excommunication of Martin Luther and the trial of Joan of Arc. It even contains Galileo's signed renunciation of his belief that the Earth revolved around the sun, which he made to avoid execution as a heretic. The Vatican Library is truly the smorgasbord of Western historical documents — secret and public, tragic and triumphant — gathered for well over five hundred years, often with no other copy in the world.

The sheer size of the Vatican Library is both its strength and its weakness. Even today, it is often said that some librarians can find documents that others cannot locate. In 1939–1940, there were only crude manual indexes to the ancient documents. It likely took more than a year to mine the Vatican Library for clues to Peter's death and burial, and to make other preparations.

The task began, of course, with the Bible itself, which paints a full, if conflicting, picture of Peter during Christ's life. He was both incredibly brave and cowardly, but always deeply devoted to Christ. The Bible provided important clues to the physical characteristics of Peter. He was a Jew from Palestine, a fisherman, and likely quite robust. Assuming he was roughly the same age as Christ in A.D. 30, he would have been in his sixties by 64–66, the time of Nero's persecution. If the later accounts that claimed he was crucified upside down were true, his relics would show forensic evidence not only of age, but also the great violence to which he was subjected.

The Bible, with the exception of two letters written by Peter, leaves Peter in Jerusalem in 44, almost twenty years before his death. The two much later, undated letters from Peter, believed to have been written in about 66, are clearly penned by a man on the run from persecution to followers also facing persecution and death. However, they infer Peter's presence in Babylon — a code word used by ancient Christians and Jews for evil, materialistic Rome. The Bible likewise contains the final letter of Peter's comrade, Saint Paul, clearly written from Rome while he was awaiting his execution by Nero: "… the time of my departure is at hand. I have competed well; I have finished the race; I have kept the faith" (2 Tim 4:6–7). Paul's burial site on the road to Rome's Port Ostia, just outside Rome's walls, has been continuously maintained by Christians since his death in 64–65.

Ignatius of Antioch, an early Christian who knew Peter, wrote while being brought to Rome for execution in 105 that he would be joining Peter and Paul, who were buried there. The Apostle Project excavators also located a letter written by a presbyter named Gaius around 200, responding to the boasting of a heretical leader named Proclus: "I can show you the trophies of the apostles. For, whether you go to the Vatican hill, or to the Ostian road, you will meet with the monuments of them who by their preaching and miracles founded this church."[72] By "trophies," Gaius referred to the tombs of the apostles.

In the case of Paul, Gaius's words are validated: Christians continue to honor Paul's actual grave on the Port Road. Finding the so-called Trophy of Gaius marking Peter's gravesite thus became central to the search.[73] The excavators believed that if the monument erected by early Christians and described by Gaius survived, Peter would be near or under it. To further complicate matters, however, the excavators found early writings that warned that the site of Peter's burial had been used as bait by the Romans to lure and capture Christians.[74]

Constantine's Treasure

One of the most extraordinary books of history is the *Liber Pontificalis ("Book of the Popes")*.[75] It is like a yearbook for the Catholic Church, maintained for 1,500 years. Written intermittently since before the fall of the Western Roman Empire, it contains biographies and summaries of the popes from Peter until Pope Pius II in 1464, written by a series of different authors from the fifth century forward.

This book provided definitive guidance to the Apostle Project. According to the *Liber Pontificalis*, Constantine surrounded the grave of Peter with a marble enclosure and then centered the original St. Peter's Basilica directly over Peter's remains, which were placed in a large bronze sarcophagus. Within the marble enclosure, Constantine assembled a great treasure of gold and silver objects to honor Peter. These included hundreds of pounds of golden crowns, thousands of pounds of silver objects, and other ancient artifacts. The treasure was reportedly topped by a massive, 150-pound golden cross inscribed with the name of Constantine and his mother, Helena. The *Liber Pontificalis* reportedly relied upon a letter written by Constantine himself, and it was definitive on the subject of Peter's tomb, providing exact measurements and precise dimensions.

If the *Liber Pontificalis* was correct, the excavators should be able simply to go to the center of the basilica, locate and break through Constantine's marble enclosure, and find not only Peter, but also one of history's greatest treasure troves.

Discouragingly, various authorities indicate that during the late persecutions (250–311), remains of the Christian dead lost their protected status under Roman law and were routinely desecrated and destroyed. Like the Nazis' desecration of Jewish cemeteries throughout Europe, the ancient Roman persecutors even made war on the dead. Perhaps Peter's remains had been destroyed long before the time of Constantine. Perhaps the search would turn up nothing at all.

CHAPTER NINE

INTO THE CITY OF THE DEAD

The excavations began in 1940, in the area of the tombs discovered during the burial of Pius XI. The team planned to move west toward the area directly under the center of the Vatican — the place where legend and ancient writings placed Peter's grave. It is hard to overstate the difficult conditions involved in the excavation. Overhead stood one of the largest and heaviest structures on Earth. Underneath was a totally unknown area. In between lay a gray, dusty, subterranean world filled 1,600 years before with debris. The excavation required the construction of concrete pillars to support the vast bulk of the Vatican above. Then it was slow, hard work to excavate the ancient debris underneath, piece by piece.[76]

In addition, all work had to be performed without power tools.[77] A small army of workers, sworn to secrecy, was required, given the immense magnitude of the project.[78] Unventilated, poorly lit, and incredibly hot in summer, the Necropolis was a terribly difficult place to work, particularly when required to use only crude tools. Overhead the normal work of the Vatican continued while the excavation went on silently, wholly concealed from the thousands of daily visitors. Underneath, the Ferrua team (quickly excluding Kaas from any day-to-day supervision) faced hard choices. The excavation itself on occasion required the destruction of ancient walls and monuments. The team was about to do a very hard job very badly.

It took until 1941 for the research to be completed, the team lined up, and the secret excavation to begin.[79] It is remarkable that it began at all. Outside the subterranean grottos, the Old World perished. The Nazis, joined by Mussolini's Italy, broke France's back, gaining complete control of non-Russian Europe. Brave England stood almost alone. Blackshirts marched through Rome in triumph carrying fasces in a strange imitation of the eagles of ancient Roman legions. Vatican City became a small island in a Fascist sea of fake legionaries and celebrating crowds.

Beneath the Vatican, the team almost immediately encountered other pagan tombs, traveling back in time to the height of Roman power around A.D. 150. They discovered remarkable, bright floral drawings and a large painting depicting a long-dead Roman master examining the ledgers of a servant.[80] After several weeks spent in the first new tomb, they unearthed the so-called Valerius Tomb.[81] In this classic Roman family tomb, there were statues in niches depicting various generations of the Valerius family beginning around 130.

Among statutes of pagan gods in the Valerius Tomb, the team found the first important clue that Peter's remains were near. There were crudely drawn pictures of Christ and Peter bearing the partial inscription: "Peter pray Christ Jesus for the holy...." The remainder of the inscription was missing.[82] These inscriptions, written in the middle of a second-century pagan cemetery in Rome, would have been the ancient world equivalent of Isis graffiti on the White

House today, or a cross drawn on the Shrine of Khomeini in Teheran. How they came to be or what ancient braveheart risking death wrote them was a mystery. Yet the inscriptions did provide an important confirmation that someone in the ancient world had been willing to risk death to identify this site, in the middle of a pagan cemetery in the hostile Roman capital, with Peter.[83]

Little by little, the excavation began to unravel the hidden Necropolis so long suspended in time and frozen in place. There was no hint at all in any ancient writings of the amazing world the excavators were now unlocking. No surviving authority ever mentioned that Vatican Hill had once served as the home of numerous Roman family tombs — some housing generations of Roman families stretching over two hundred years. It was apparent that a number of other magnificent, largely pagan tombs existed between the location of the Peter inscription and the center of St. Peter's Basilica. Moreover, the Ferrua team quickly realized that there were other parallel streets with parallel tombs on other sides. The team was working in a second-century Roman city of the dead containing hundreds of memorials from the height of power of the Roman Empire.[84]

In fact, the team had uncovered a totally forgotten collection of the legendary family tombs of Rome, like those that had once also lined the Appian Way. But unlike the Appian Way tombs, which survived only in written descriptions and ruins, these family tombs were wholly intact, frozen in time since 337, well before the barbarian invasions. The destroyed tombs along the Appian Way had commemorated the greatest and most ancient families of Rome, but the family tombs in the Necropolis commemorated the "newer men" who ascended to power or prosperity after A.D. 100. They chronicled in murals, busts, and the like, the history of the Classic Age of the Roman Empire. Because they had been forgotten, they survived the vast barbarian invasions that plunged Europe into darkness. The tombs were magnificent — an astounding archeological find. But they were not Peter's grave. The great question remained whether Peter would be found.

The excavators believed that once they reached the center, they would find a large bronze sarcophagus with Peter inside, based on the fifth-century account. It made sense to Ferrua that Constantine would have honored Peter in this way. Ferrua and Kaas were anxious to skip the intervening pagan tombs and proceed as rapidly as possible to the center. Kaas, however, the nominal leader of the project, was much disturbed by the destruction caused by Ferrua's excavation. In particular, he was deeply troubled by the nonchalance with which the Ferrua team treated the human remains they encountered.[85]

Kaas' disquiet was well justified. Even allowing for the difficult conditions, the Ferrua team ignored basic accepted archeological precautions. Few photographs were taken of the numerous murals and inscriptions they encountered — artifacts of incalculable value. In fact, no comprehensive photographic record was made. No effort was made to preserve the colored murals and inscriptions. Given their exposure to the damp and dirty atmosphere after two thousand years of burial under rubble, fading was inevitable without preservation. How much was lost will never be known. Inscriptions of profound meaning were dismissed as incomprehensible gibberish. Human remains were ignored or bundled up and stored away without any contemporaneous examination by medical anthropologists.[86] After the excavation of two more large family tombs filled with wonderful portraits of swans in purple fields, pictures of Hercules, and a masterpiece mosaic of Pluto, the god of the dead, on a chariot, as well as the ashes and busts of centuries of ancestors,[87] Kaas called a temporary halt to the excavation of new tombs and the race to the center. He insisted on a cleanup and cataloging of the excavated areas.

The Ferrua team used the pause to excavate a dirt passageway.[88] Under a small slab, they stumbled into another shocking surprise — a small, hidden underground tomb from about A.D. 250, containing remarkable Christian images of Jonah and the whale, the Good Shepherd, a fisherman, and the resurrected Christ in a heavenly chariot.[89] These were among the earliest surviving depictions of these Christian stories. The physical depiction of these stories within a few hundred yards of the seat of Roman power was an amazing act of courage by an unknown, talented artist, who risked horrible death for creating these Christian images. It was a remarkable find, but it did not reference Peter in any way.

So far, the Ferrua team had only found the single earlier reference to Peter. Yet the team realized that Constantine faced immense difficulty in his attempt to center the first St. Peter's basilica over an exact spot on Vatican Hill, requiring massive fill and the desecration of a centuries-old cemetery.[90] There were many other much easier, more level building sites within a short distance. Constantine would have undertaken such a difficult and elaborate building project only to center the basilica directly over Peter's grave. Moreover, as the team moved deeper into the Necropolis, they noticed an astounding fact. The Roman engineers had cropped tombs and added fill to center the altar of the basilica directly over an exact and precise center point, not at the hill's original top.[91] Surely Constantine would only have gone to such extensive effort if the grave of Saint Peter was the exact center point.

Kaas met with Pius XII and outlined the findings. Pius then ordered the project to proceed directly into the underground center of St. Peter's — the legendary grave of Peter. He insisted that the project remain in absolute secrecy. The world would know nothing at all of the project for ten years.

CHAPTER TEN

INSIDE THE TOMB

As 1941 rolled into 1942, the Ferrua team determined to begin excavation in the exact area where the ancient writings reported the original basilica stood over Peter's tomb. Based on the ancient accounts, Kaas and his team believed they would find Peter's remains in a glorious bronze sarcophagus created by Constantine to honor Peter.[92] A monument to mark the tomb, called the Trophy of Gaius, had reportedly been erected around 150 or earlier, but completely covered four times over the millennia — during the building of the first basilica by Constantine and then in 600, in the twelfth century, and in the seventeenth century.[93] The team believed they would find the Trophy of Gaius near Constantine's bronze sarcophagus.

Outside, the world remained oblivious to these secret excavations. Millions died in Germany's invasion of Russia, and the Axis powers spread over the globe. Mussolini strutted before huge crowds outside Vatican City. The Italian conquerors, with Nazi help, reached El Alamein in the Western Desert of Egypt and threatened Britain's lifeline — the Suez Canal. Likewise, the Italians, with German help, conquered Yugoslavia, Greece, and Rhodes. Christianity was an irrelevant afterthought to the cheering Fascist crowds. Meanwhile, America was finally awakened from its sleep by Pearl Harbor.

Under the Vatican, the excavators began to work directly over the place where legend and writings placed Peter's burial two thousand years before. The team found themselves among numerous first- and second-century Roman tombs. Several of these dated back almost to the death of Peter and the Age of Nero. But in the very center of the Necropolis, they encountered one of history's strangest structures. It was a maze of shrines within shrines and walls within walls, resembling a set of Russian matryoshka dolls, one nesting inside the other, each smaller shrine older than the larger one that housed it.[94] What actually lay underneath each layer was a mystery. Tunneling into the center involved destroying portions of ancient shrines, but the excavators proceeded anyway, traveling back hundreds of years in time as they neared the center. They encountered first a magnificent, Renaissance-era altar from the early 1600s. It had been built to cover earlier altars during the construction of the new St. Peter's. Moving through this, they found a smaller altar built between 1119 and 1124.[95] In effect, they traveled back to the age of the Crusades — the age of Saladin and Richard.

Finally, as 1942 rolled on, they encountered two important walls. The first, called the Red Wall, was made of red bricks from the time of the Emperor Marcus Aurelius. It was therefore dated after, but near, 160. This wall transected the area.[96] Why or how the Red Wall was built remained a mystery. A second wall, which became known as the Graffiti Wall, built around 250, was also located near the Necropolis's center.[97] This wall, cut off by later construction, was covered in markings. The marks were clearly Roman names and symbols, but they were otherwise unreadable to the Ferrua team, who dismissed the wall as unintelligible and insignificant.[98]

The dismissal of the inscriptions on the Graffiti Wall would turn out to be a disastrous mistake.

There were other mistakes as well. In the rush to find the bronze sarcophagus, Ferrua largely ignored the other human remains the team periodically encountered. The field of forensic study of human remains for historical purposes was largely undeveloped at this time. It probably never occurred to the Ferrua team that the remains themselves could provide valuable evidence. The team ignored Kaas, the project leader, when he urged greater respect for the dead. Eventually they refused to speak to him, treating him with cold contempt as an amateur among professionals. Kaas, however, would quietly return to the excavation site each day after work, where he would recover and respectfully box the remains that Ferrua and his team had passed over in their hurry.[99] He did so more as a priest than an archeologist. He would then label and date the remains, citing the location where they were found, and give the bones to a workman to place in storage. Ultimately, Ferrua's blindness to the Graffiti Wall and his indifference to human remains would delay for decades the discovery of the true story of Saint Peter.

Margherita Guarducci

A short distance away, now also in Rome, Margherita Guarducci completed her work deciphering Cretian and pre-Classical Greek inscriptions, three hundred to five thousand years old. She had discovered and photographed these over many years in remote locations on the island of Crete, now occupied by the Nazis. Interrupted by the war, she moved to Rome, where she taught at the University of Rome. She had no idea of the work going on under the Vatican. However, Guarducci would in several years become involved, using her extraordinary powers of deduction to see what Ferrua was too blind to see.

Some people are endowed with special, inexplicable gifts of genius — for example, George Strake's second sight, which enabled him to see the hidden ocean of oil where others only saw dirt and undrinkable water. These gifts manifest themselves in strange ways. Young Willie Mays runs at the crack of a bat to the exact spot in the vast center field of the Polo Grounds where the ball will land. An aging, paunchy Babe Ruth hits fifty-four home runs in 1928 — twice as many as any other player — because he has an instinct that tells him where and how the pitch will come. Vincent van Gogh sees the stars we all see, but his *Starry Night* shows us something we never imagined. A deaf Beethoven composes the Ninth Symphony, carrying those of us who can hear to heights we never could have dreamed of. In the same way, Guarducci had a strange genius of her own. She was consumed by inscription puzzles, and she had a special sight — a combination of deduction and genius — that would allow her in time to decipher the clues leading to Peter.

No Bronze Sarcophagus, No Great Golden Cross

But that was decades away. For now, through wall after wall, Ferrua's team continued to excavate. They worked through an eleventh-century shrine erected in the Age of the Crusades and the Norman Conquest. They then encountered a smaller altar built by Pope Saint Gregory the Great around 600, when the Western world lay largely in darkness — a relic of the Dark Ages. Now came the greatest point of suspense so far in the excavation: Would they uncover the marble enclosure built by Constantine within the Gregory altar? If so would it actually be intact, or would it simply house another looted tomb?

On the windy plain outside the ancient ruins of Ephesus in Turkey lies the tomb of the Apostle John — the "beloved" apostle. This tomb was once the centerpiece of a great church also built by Constantine. Now John's grave is an empty hole amid ruins, looted long ago by Saracens and then Venetians. Would Peter's grave be simply another looted hole? Breaking through Gregory's altar, the team found the marble enclosure built by Constantine exactly as described in the *Book of the Popes*; it was wholly intact. It had never been entered in the nearly 1,700 years since it was sealed.

The team was elated, convinced they were on the verge of uncovering the great gold cross and bronze sarcophagus described in the *Book of the Popes*. They were about to be the first humans in 1,600 years to see Constantine's monument to Peter. They broke into the Constantine enclosure, exposing it for the first time since 337. They were shocked both by what was there and what was missing. No great bronze sarcophagus. No large gold cross. No gold or silver of any kind. Instead, what they found was a strange second-century monument, not at all Christian in form but actually in a pagan style, but clearly a marker. Could this monument be the fabled Trophy of Gaius? If so, did Peter and the great treasure lie within or under it?

In their anxiety to reach the sarcophagus, the excavators noted, but did not understand, a strange architectural detail. In a perfectly symmetrical church, built by the Romans — history's greatest engineering perfectionists — the Constantine enclosure was built asymmetrically, larger on one side than the other, so as to enclose a part of the Graffiti Wall. The Graffiti Wall had no apparent function. It would have been logical and simple for Constantine's builders to demolish it and erect a perfect enclosure for Peter's tomb. But the Romans had not done so. Instead, they created an asymmetrical structure to enclose and protect it. The excavators noted this imperfection but dismissed it as meaningless.

The Ferrua Team believed the strange marker they had discovered in the Constantine enclosure to be the legendary Trophy of Gaius.[100] Nearby tiles bearing inscriptions from the Emperor Aurelius indicated the monument dated to about A.D. 150. Many coins (one dating to A.D. 14) and Christian votive offerings were found.[101] The monument's pagan appearance had probably been intended to conceal its purpose from Roman officials. A cross or Christian symbol in the Roman capitol would have been quickly destroyed and its builders crucified for their sacrilege of Rome.

Having arrived at last at the center of the Necropolis and directly under the Vatican altar, the excavators entered the Trophy of Gaius.[102] There they found wonderful murals of saints, confirming the monument's Christian origin.[103] The team was terribly disappointed, however. Inside there were no bronze sarcophagus, no great golden cross, no gold or silver, and no reference at all to Peter. They then dug down. They found an additional chamber filled with early Roman coins and votive offerings, suggesting offerings made in honor of a saint. Finally, they found a small opening near the very base of the Red Wall ... and in that opening, they encountered bones.[104]

Pius XII was summoned. He watched as the bones were exhumed from their dusty grave. Everyone watching believed that after two thousand years, they had found the remains of Peter. Yet they were perplexed by the absence of the bronze casket and treasure described in the *Book of the Popes*. Why had the great apostle been interred in a simple dirt grave instead of under a golden cross or other more fitting monument? Perhaps the builders of the first St. Peter's Basilica had not wished to disturb the apostle's initial grave. This explanation satisfied the Ferrua team. They believed the numerous ancient coins and votive offerings in the vicinity of the grave were sufficient to prove its authenticity.

It was 1942. The bones were placed in lead-lined boxes at the pope's direction and moved to his own apartment, where they would rest for many years. His personal physician (a general practitioner untrained in forensics) examined the remains and declared them to be those of a sixty-five-year-old man.[105] The more than two thousand coins discovered on the floor of Peter's grave were found to date to the first and second centuries, close to the time of Peter's death. Graves of other early popes were found in close proximity. Moreover, it was clear these bones had been buried before the Red Wall was built around 160.[106] All were convinced that they had found the relics of Peter. The later discovery of the graves of other early popes seemed to confirm the finding. At the express command of Pius XII, the find was to be kept absolutely secret.

In truth, the excavators had made a logical, but terrible, mistake — one that would not be discovered for a decade. Just like the pagan Romans long ago, the excavators were blind to certain key clues, ingeniously designed to protect Peter's remains from discovery. For now, the excavations financed by Strake continued while the war raged on outside.

CHAPTER ELEVEN

THE THREE AMIGOS

While Pius XII may have erred in choosing an internal archeological team without outside consultants, he made no mistake at all in picking his external team to deal with financing the excavation and eventually with other equally grave matters. This astoundingly talented team of three priests — we'll call them the Three Amigos — accomplished amazing things far beyond the excavation of the Vatican Necropolis.

The Three Amigos possessed an extraordinary collection of talent. Monsignor Giovanni Montini, Pius XII's secretary and closest confidant, and also George Strake's friend, was the chairman and glue of this extraordinary team. Together the three men served as the pope's team on a variety of secret, sometimes very dangerous, projects. Montini was the consummate Vatican insider, spending — against his wishes — almost all of his career inside its confining walls. He was incredibly brilliant but selfless, requesting over and over that he not be promoted as he was dragged up a road that would ultimately lead to the papacy. He was bitterly hated by the Fascists, and Mussolini in particular, who resented Montini's efforts, both open and secret, on behalf of refugees. Those efforts began in 1936 after Mussolini's attack of butchery on the ancient Christian kingdom of Ethiopia.

Montini was somewhat introverted, unlike most of his papal predecessors and successors, but he had a deep love of history and commitment to peace. He was fascinated by and loved the United States from his earliest Vatican days, and he learned English to better understand that strange country whose freedom so contrasted with old Europe and the confining walls of the Vatican. It was probably this fascination that caused Montini to recruit two young American priests as his ablest assistants and closest comrades in the early 1940s: Walter Carroll and Joseph McGeough. His love for and knowledge of the United States was almost certainly responsible for Montini sending Carroll on an unlikely journey to visit George Strake in Houston.

Walter Carroll, only thirty years old when he visited Strake, was a deeply engaging man with impeccable social skills and a smile that lit up any room. Tall and dark-haired, he had a commanding but inviting presence. He was a native of Pittsburgh, where both of his brothers were also priests. He suffered from terrible coronary illness from childhood and at times required months of rest simply to regain normal strength. His condition marked him for an early death, so he lived life with frenetic energy and a desperate courage beyond bravery. His friends said simply he had *joie de vivre*, an incredible love of each moment of life. He met and dealt not only with Strake, but with President Franklin D. Roosevelt and Generals Mark Clark, George Patton, and Dwight D. Eisenhower, and many others, whose confidence he commanded.[107] Although a priest, he had the larcenous heart of a riverboat gambler, concocting or participating in a variety of outrageous scams to defeat the Nazis and save the Jews — the discovery of any of which would have brought his execution.[108] Carroll's friends said he walked with kings but had the common touch. He was Montini's closest friend and comrade. He was consumed, like Montini, with aiding the victims of persecution. While aiding refugees, he conveyed important intelligence information to the Allies — serving as a spy for the Church.[109]

The third of the amigos was Joseph McGeough, only thirty-seven years old when he joined Montini and Carroll. While deeply religious, he had all of the moxie and street smarts of his birthplace of Manhattan — land of Jay Gould, J. P. Morgan, Bernie Madoff, and many others. Tall and dark-haired, McGeough had uncommon brass, but largely avoided any public persona, even writing letters under the code name "Father Fitzsimmons." The schemes he conceived with Carroll and Montini would save countless thousands of lives during World War II. In later years, McGeough would go public and become the Vatican's go-to emissary in crisis areas — to an Ethiopia ravaged by Mussolini, to South Africa to combat apartheid in 1960, and to Ireland in 1966 to combat civil unrest over religious differences.

In mid-1943, however, the Three Amigos faced challenges much closer to home. Immediate problems intruded upon the excavation beneath the Vatican. It was becoming increasingly questionable whether the Vatican itself, the city of Rome, and Italy's Jewish population would survive at all. It was the Three Amigos the pope would employ in this crisis.

CHAPTER TWELVE

THE WAR

While Pius kept secret the great discoveries going on beneath the Vatican, World War II exploded into the deadliest conflict in human history. After initial Axis victories, the tide turned in favor of the Allies at El Alamein in the North African desert, the Naval Battle of Midway in the Central Pacific, and bloody Stalingrad in the Russian winter. The victory parades in Rome by Blackshirts carrying fasces around the Colosseum in imitation of the Roman legions disappeared. Mussolini was no Julius Caesar, and the Italian troops were no Roman legions; they died by the tens of thousands in North Africa and Russia. Death, hunger, and disease stalked every corner and almost every family in Rome.

The Church remained neutral — with a wink. Churches and priests throughout Europe were at the mercy of Nazi fanatics, with hundreds already imprisoned at Dachau (along with tens of thousands of Jews). To protect her own, the Church maintained a pretense of neutrality while riding a tiger. In reality the Church secretly carried out a number of efforts to aid the Allies and thwart Nazi power. Although Pius and the Three Amigos remained in secret contact with George Strake during the war years, their respective circumstances could not have been more different.

The Strakes — The War Years

During the war, Strake's Conroe Field was an important ingredient in fueling the Allied war effort. The Conroe Field produced five hundred million barrels[110] of crude oil, the life blood fueling Allied planes, ships, and tanks around the globe. A special pipeline — the so-called Big Inch — was built to carry it and other Texas oil to refineries in the East and then to Europe. Strake's immense revenues continued to be contributed in substantial part to the pope's causes. The field also enriched Conroe and formed the basis of the wealth of many others, leading to the discovery of many other smaller oil fields in similar strata in east Texas.

Strake's restless soul also led him to wildcat in remote areas in other states. Although he enjoyed considerable success in locating new oil fields, neither he nor anyone else would ever duplicate the unexpected success of the Conroe Field.

Before World War II, the late-1930s movie *Lost Horizons* (based on a 1933 James Hilton best seller) described a valley called Shangri La in the Himalayan mountains that provided a refuge of peace for a World War I veteran from a world that was about to destroy itself in another war. As it turned out, the movie foreshadowed the coming of a second world war. In the mountains of Colorado before World War II broke out, George Strake found the house that would become his haven from the world: his own Shangri La. Long before, while he was on leave from the Army during World War I, George had traveled to Colorado. Like so many others, he fell in love with it, vowing to his best friend that someday he would "buy a mountain."

In the late 1930s, he found and purchased a unique mountain valley called Glen Eyrie, near Colorado Springs and the Garden of the Gods. The 1,200-acre property had been developed in the gilded age of the 1880s and 1890s by a railroad magnate named William Palmer. As a tribute to his deceased wife and in fulfillment of a promise to her, Palmer built a large Tudor-style castle on the property. (Think of a bigger, better Downton Abbey.) It had been neglected for many years since Palmer's death by a variety of owners. Strake restored it, turning it into an astounding summer place, its Queen Canyon rivaling in natural beauty the Maroon Bells Valley near Aspen. Its waterfalls, lake, and wildlife made it a summer heaven for the Strakes and their friends escaping hot, humid Houston. George added a more intimate house — the so-called Pink House — for his family and guests, and even added a bowling alley in the massive foyer of the main building. Although Strake would later sell the property for a nominal price to a Christian group, during the summers of the 1940s, it was the Strake family paradise. As the world once again turned to catastrophic war, Glen Eyrie was an oasis of peace.

The Strakes, perhaps not surprisingly, were never direct friends of Howard Hughes — in those days, not the decrepit recluse of later years, but rather the brilliant founder of the early airline TWA and movie producer. Because they both had strong oilfield and Houston ties and were among the wealthiest people in the United States, however, they had many common friends, both in Houston and among Hollywood movie stars.

The deep Catholic faith of the Strake family contrasted with their immense wealth and sometimes created dilemmas for the Strake children. In 1943, Howard Hughes released the film *The Outlaw*, highlighting Jane Russell's busty cleavage. Hughes said there are two good reasons for any man to see Jane Russell in a movie, while Bob Hope called the movie star "the two and only Jane Russell." The Catholic Church condemned the movie, declaring it a mortal sin to see it — a sin of sufficient gravity to cause the loss of salvation. When the young Strake kids were introduced to Jane Russell and other stars of *The Outlaw* by their parents at Glen Eyrie, they were terrified the entire family was risking eternal damnation.

The peace of Glen Eyrie with its waterfalls, quiet canyons, wildlife, and nearby Eagle Lake, could not have contrasted more vividly with the increasing desperation of Rome and its endangered Jews.

July 1943

The Allies destroyed the Italian and German armies in North Africa and then reached across the Mediterranean to Sicily. The spectacle of Italian crowds in Palermo and other cities wildly cheering the arrival of U.S. General Patton caused the Italian military to depose and imprison Mussolini. Walter Carroll led a team of Allied military officers to Rome, arriving at 2:30 a.m. to receive in secret the surrender of Italy from the new Italian government.[111] The Germans struck first, however, before the nighttime surrender could take effect. Freeing Mussolini in a bold raid led by the Waffen-SS, the Germans set up a puppet Italian government and seized control of their former ally.

Strangely paralleling the activities of Nero, a new monster strolled in and took control of the Eternal City after the collapse of Mussolini's government in July 1943. Adolf Hitler, like Nero, targeted a religious minority — the Jews. His minions wreaked their cruelty not in public arenas, but mostly in less public concentration camps. It was the same base, cruel execution of men, women, and children made even more widespread and sinister by modern communications and the use of modern technology to create an assembly line of death for millions of innocent people. The Nazis began a roundup of Italy's large Jewish population for deportation to concentration camps in the North, where most of them faced extermination. The ancient Jewish population of Rome and Italy was targeted for death.

The Refugee Bureau

The Three Amigos hit upon a happy scheme to deceive the Nazis, while paradoxically aiding Axis prisoners of war. After the catastrophic German losses in North Africa and Sicily, the Allies held several hundred thousand German and Italian prisoners, including the remnants of Rommel's Africa Corps as well as many Italian civilians interned in Libya. Montini placed Carroll and McGeough in a special Vatican Refugee Bureau ostensibly to aid the Germans and Italians held by the Allies. The choice of two Americans to lead the Bureau seemed logical to the Nazis and Fascists, as they would be best able to deal with their fellow Americans who held most of the prisoners and internees. They did actually aid the Axis prisoners, but this (unknown to the Nazis) was only a small part of what they did. The true aim of the Refugee Bureau was to save the Jews and Rome, while aiding the Allies. The Bureau provided a cover for Carroll and McGeough to cross Allied lines and actually meet with Allied leaders. They also used the Bureau to aid refugees the Nazis did not have in mind — Jewish refugees and escaped Allied POWs. Much of the Vatican Refugee Bureau's funding came from Catholic Charities USA, whose largest funder was George Strake. (He joined the Executive Committee of Catholic Charities in 1940, following Walter Carroll's visit.) Drawing also upon virtually unlimited financing deposited in a bank in Pittsburgh, Pennsylvania, Carroll and Montini embarked upon dangerous schemes to aid the Allies, save Rome, and save as many Italian Jews as possible, still using the Refugee Bureau as a cover.[112]

Carroll and McGeough exchanged their United States passports for Vatican passports, repeatedly crossing enemy lines to bring intelligence and requests for Rome's preservation from Pope Pius XII to General Mark Clark, commander in Italy, and General Walter Bedell Smith, Eisenhower's Chief of Staff.[113] The two priests were virtually the only Americans in Rome — an enemy capital. On at least one occasion, Carroll carried Pius's message directly to Washington, D.C., and met with President Franklin D. Roosevelt for two and a half hours. Discovery of these activities would have brought execution.[114]

Saving Rome

In July 1943, more than nine hundred Allied bombers attacked the rail yards in Rome, which were being used to support Axis troops in the south, killing more than 4,500 Romans. This was one of only two Allied air raids on Rome — the other was a pilot error — which together caused thousands of deaths in 1943 and 1944. McGeough and Montini worked directly with "Wild Bill" Donovan, head of the United States' OSS (later the CIA) to reduce or eliminate casualties, while rescuing both the Jews and downed Allied pilots. Meanwhile, Nazi storm troopers ruled Italy, with the SS rounding up Jews and many others for transportation to extermination camps.

Montini, Carroll, and McGeough labored to dissuade the Americans from further attacks on the Eternal City. Rome was the Germans' logistical and transportation base. In a real sense, all roads led to Rome. An important part of the mission of the Three Amigos was to dissuade the Americans from taking the logical military step of destroying the Germans' logistical and transportation center by bombing Rome. In effect, they had to ask for the terrible sacrifice of enduring thousands of Allied casualties to preserve the Eternal City.

The Allied invasion at Salerno in Italy's toe led only to a slow, bloody Allied advance north along the Italian Boot, so the Allies determined to strike directly at Rome through massive landings at Anzio in central Italy, less than forty miles from Rome. The Anzio landing on January 22, 1944, miscarried. The Allies were bottled up in a small beachhead perimeter — sitting ducks for the German artillery. Winston Churchill described the invasion as a great whale beached on the sand. For three long months until late May 1944, the pinned-down Allies suffered 43,000 casualties, some of their greatest single casualties of the war — vastly greater than those who would later die on the beaches of Normandy. Two Ranger Battalions lost 761 out of 767 men. It was the most disastrous Allied landing of World War II. The Nazis marched Allied prisoners captured at Anzio to Rome. There they photographed them in staged marches past the Colosseum, surrounded by Nazi soldiers, a publicity stunt designed to humiliate the United States.

Carroll's trips back and forth across the warring lines took a terrible toll on him. His travels took him to Washington to meet with FDR for several hours, and he took several trips to Algiers to meet with Allied leaders. He went to the dangerous Anzio beachhead to minister to and share the suffering of the Allied troops trapped and dying there by the thousands. All the while he forwarded intelligence reports from behind German lines to General Mark Clark and his staff. In April 1944, Carroll suffered a major heart attack at Anzio, nearly ending his life. In typical fashion, as soon as he could stand again, although gray, weak, and frail, he renewed his activities, meeting with Clark and Eisenhower's chief of staff, Bedell Smith, to aid the Allies, save the Jews, and preserve the city of Rome.[115]

Against all odds, Rome was not destroyed like so many other ancient cities of Western Europe — Cologne, Warsaw, Kiev, Hamburg, and others, which did not survive the ravages of World War II. Walter Carroll was largely responsible. As General Mark Clark, Allied Commander in Italy, later said, "Without the helpfulness and intelligence of Carroll, the outcome in Italy would have been much different."[116] Also without Carroll's efforts, it is likely that the Necropolis would have become a buried afterthought in a new set of ruins produced by modern warfare.

Rome was and is the Eternal City. The city contains the physical remains of more than two thousand years of Western civilization, from the Romans through the Dark and Middle Ages to the Renaissance. Beyond its significance to Christians and Italians, it stands at the heart of much of Western history and culture from the Roman Republic through the Middle Ages and the Renaissance. With its collection of buildings like the Pantheon, the Colosseum, the Forum, and its works of art like the Trevi Fountain, the Spanish Steps, the statues of Bernini, the Sistine Chapel, and the *Pietà* of Michelangelo, Rome is truly the legacy of mankind.

On June 3, 1944, Walter Carroll's mother was interviewed by the Pittsburgh Press. Asked whether she was anxious for her son since Rome was about to fall, she said she was not, as she was sure he would be nowhere close. She must have been quite surprised to learn the truth. General Clark entered Rome in June 1944 with Eisenhower's chief of staff, Bedell Smith, riding in a Jeep guided by Walter Carroll, en route to meet directly with Pope Pius

XII. Carroll was noticeably gray. The photo of their entry into Rome became one of the iconic photos of World War II, published even in Pittsburgh. Mrs. Carroll's reaction upon seeing it is unknown.

In addition to saving Rome from the advancing Allies, the Vatican had an equally difficult task of preventing Rome's destruction by the retreating Germans. Pius and Kaas negotiated with Catholic German generals to designate Rome as an "open city" — apparently in direct violation of an order from Hitler to SS General Karl Wolff to seize the Vatican and Pope Pius XII.

Saving the Jews

Equally as difficult as saving Rome was saving Italy's ancient Jewish population. Here Montini, Carroll, and McGeough again played leading roles.[117] For example, on the outskirts of Rome, the Church owned a dilapidated estate called the Janiculum Hill Property, with a building named Casa San Giovanni[118] as its centerpiece. This served as a dormitory for Jews and other refugees in a "labyrinth of underground rooms and tunnels ventilated by shafts hidden by the outside shrubbery."[119] The property had been acquired by the Church with Strake's financing for use by North American Catholic organizations prior to World War II. It was directly across from a building occupied by the Gestapo.[120] Much like an underground railroad, Carroll and McGeough hid more than one hundred of Rome's Jews there at a time during the Holocaust, along with 1,200 sheep bought to provide agricultural cover.[121] They disguised the Jewish refugees, sometimes mixed with downed Allied pilots, as shepherds. (There is no record of how well the Allied pilots actually performed as shepherds.) The stories of the so-called Roman Escape Line, along which Allied prisoners of war were shepherded through Rome (often in cassocks) to Allied lines farther south, are the stuff of legend.

Carroll engaged in a bevy of other schemes and scams to save Italy's Jews — ranging from hiding them in the bottom levels of ancient Roman catacombs to dressing them in cassocks.[122] Another person working with Montini on this operation was Father Hugh O'Flaherty, a fiery Irishman known as the Irish Pimpernel for his activities and schemes in defeating the SS and saving the Jews.[123] When the SS placed a death warrant on O'Flaherty's head and drew a white line across St. Peter's Square to mark the boundary beyond which priests would be killed for such activities, the Refugee Bureau continued with its schemes from inside the Vatican itself.

While the Nazis captured and killed several hundred thousand Italian Jews, a substantial majority of Jews in Italy were saved — a feat not achieved in any other European country. Carroll's biographer, George Kemon, stated that the Vatican was responsible for saving some 850,000 Jews, "more than all other religious groups and relief organizations combined."[124] At all times, Carroll drew upon seemingly unlimited and mysterious funds from a bank in his hometown of Pittsburgh.

At war's end, the Allies liberated tens of thousands of starving, diseased prisoners in the terrible concentration camps at Dachau and Buchenwald. Within twenty-four hours of their liberation, Walter Carroll and Joseph McGeough arrived first at Dachau and then at Buchenwald with convoys of food, medical supplies, and more than fifty medical personnel.[125] In at least six other concentration camps, the Refugee Bureau appeared soon after liberation, saving many thousands of victims of the Nazis. Given the horrific starvation and terrible medical condition of the inmates, it is clear thousands would have died without the timely relief provided by the Bureau. There is no way to estimate the incalculable number of lives saved by these activities. An Italian inmate of Dachau at the time of Carroll's arrival would later write of their despair turning to joy upon seeing Carroll's caravan.[126]

Carroll's activities were the stuff of legend, and stories about them multiplied. One story circulating shortly after World War II concerned the legendary, irascible General George S. Patton. Patton seized a Catholic seminary in Germany to use as a military headquarters, throwing the German seminarians onto the street. Carroll traveled to Patton's headquarters to confront him, demanding return of the seminary to the Church. At first General Patton refused. A war was in progress! But Carroll challenged him again with a divine power even greater than the mighty Third Army, and crusty George Patton surrendered for the only time during World War II, telling his aides to "turn that damn building back to the pope."[127] To Patton's discomfort, Carroll stayed in the southern German castle that Patton was using as headquarters until the order was actually carried out.[128]

War's End

The Catholic Church has various Papal Orders that may be awarded to laymen to recognize their contributions to the Church and the world. The highest of these is the Order of St. Sylvester, named after the pope who reigned during the construction of the original St. Peter's Basilica, circa 330. Within the Order there are various ranks, the very highest of which is Knight Commander — the highest possible recognition of a layman by the Catholic Church. There are only a handful of living recipients of this honor. In July 1944 (immediately after the liberation of Rome), Wild Bill Donovan, head of the American OSS and later the CIA, was presented this honor by Pope Pius XII to recognize his efforts with Walter Carroll to save Rome from destruction. In 1946, George Strake was likewise made a Knight Commander of St. Sylvester, receiving the recognition in person from Pope Pius himself. This is an honor conferred on laymen of extraordinary merit, such as Oskar Schindler of *Schindler's List* fame, who was later presented the same honor.

CHAPTER THIRTEEN

THE FLOOD AND THE CURSE

The Church and the Communists

Following the defeat of the Axis Powers in 1945, a tremendous conflict broke out in Italy between the Communists and the democratic parties for postwar control of Italy. Pius XII had seen the massive persecution of the Eastern European Church, as well as the Catholic Church in China, Spain, and elsewhere, by the Communists. He had personally witnessed and nearly been killed in a 1919 massacre by the Communists in Munich. He was deeply alarmed that the Communists were filling the vacuum left in Italy by the Fascists. To counteract the Communists, Pius XII constructed church schools and family centers in the heart of devastated urban areas with a strong Communist presence. The schools would not only serve a humanitarian purpose, but would also combat the otherwise omnipresent Communist party, providing an alternative to Communism. Turning once again to Montini, McGeough, Carroll, and Strake, the Church began construction of church schools and family centers in poor, largely Communist areas.[129]

Garbatella, an impoverished neighborhood in the south of Rome, is the subject of an Italian political proverb: "As goes Garbatella, so goes Rome. As goes Rome, so goes Italy." So the very first church the Three Amigos and Strake built was Saint Philip Neri in Garbatella. In a country full of spectacular but increasingly empty cathedrals, this new church was smaller and family-oriented, modeled on the more vigorous American churches. Unlike the great cathedrals, it was not simply a place of worship, but a center for education and many family activities. This was the pope's answer to the Communists. Based on its success, more than thirty-eight other family-oriented churches were quickly built throughout Italy. The postwar Catholic Church in Italy was reinvigorated by these new churches.

In the 1948 Italian elections, the Communist Party sought to take power. *Time* magazine said Italy was "on the brink of catastrophe."[130] The Communists had just seized Czechoslovakia in a February 1948 coup. Poland, Hungary, Romania, and the Baltic States were all occupied, and Berlin was blockaded by Stalin's order and kept alive only by an American airlift. It appeared that all of Western Europe might crumble to Stalin. Had the Communists taken power in Italy, it would likely have outflanked and destroyed NATO. It is probable that the future of Europe hung in the balance based on the outcome of the 1948 Italian elections. A Communist victory was avoided after Pius XII spoke against the party. The Communists carried much of Northern Italy but were crushed everywhere else. The old proverb proved true: Garbatella voted against the Communists, followed by Rome and the rest of Italy. At least one contemporary newspaper account attributed the

Portrait of George Strake

George Strake with drilling
crew on Well No. 2

Explosion of the Conroe Field
at Crater Hill, 1933

George Strake's magnificent Glen Eyrie Castle in Colorado

George Strake with Frank Sinatra, Phil Silvers, and Dorothy Lamour, 1951

ABOVE: Pope Pius XII
at prayer

ABOVE RIGHT: Eugenio
Pacelli, the future Pope
Pius XII, as a young boy

RIGHT: American
prisoners of war from
Anzio being paraded
through Rome by
the Nazi soldiers, c. 1944

Monsignor Walter Carroll (on the right) and Monsignor McGeough in the Vatican gardens, June 26, 1944. *Credit: National Archives and Records Administration, College Park, MD - 111-C-2018*

Monsignor Giovanni Battista Montini, the future Pope Paul VI, with Pope Pius XII, 1947. *Credit: Religious News Service, OSV archive*

U.S. General Mark Clark entered Rome in triumph on June 4, 1944. He stopped at the Vatican to greet Pope Pius XII. Shown here in St. Peter's Square. *Credit: Wikimedia Commons*

Pope Pius XII prays at the tomb of Saint Peter. *Credit: Religious News Service, OSV archive*

Pope Paul VI with George Strake, 1960

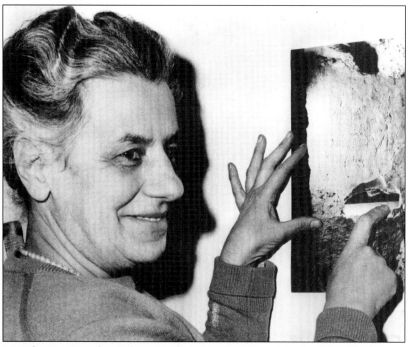
Margherita Guarducci shows a photograph of the niche in the wall where the bones believed to be the Apostle Peter's were originally found. *Credit: Religious News Service, OSV archive*

Margherita Guarducci in her home. *Credit: OSV archive*

Tombs uncovered during excavation of the Vatican Necropolis

TOP: Tombs of the Valeri. *Credit: OSV archive*

LEFT: Vatican Necropolis, dirt road that runs between the tombs under the Vatican. *Credit: courtesy of Fabbrica di San Pietro, Vatican*

Fragment of the Red Wall bearing inscriptions decoded by Margherita Guarducci, revealing the location of the Apostle Peter. The graffiti on this fragment reads "Petros eni." *Credit: Courtesy of Fabbrica di San Pietro, Vatican*

Roman tomb discovered beneath the Vatican known as the Tomb of the Chariot. *Credit: Courtesy of Fabbrica di San Pietro, Vatican*

Pope Francis holds the relics of the Apostle Peter during a Mass in St. Peter's Square, November 24, 2013. *Credit: Newscom, REUTERS/Stefano Rellandini*

Pope Francis prays for deceased popes at the altar built above the tomb of Saint Peter in the Vatican grottoes beneath the high altar of St. Peter's Basilica, November 2, 2014. *Credit: Newscom*

salvation of Italy to Montini and "the three Americans" — Strake, Carroll, and McGeough.[131]

The Italian Church itself enjoyed a new burst of energy for a time, engaging with families through these new churches. At Saint Philip Neri in Garbatella, portraits of George Strake and Walter Carroll today sit side by side, a testimony to their great contribution. (Strake in his portrait wears a quizzical look, perhaps wondering how a Texas Wildcatter ended up in Garbatella.)

Through all the years of clever maneuvering by the Three Amigos and turmoil with the Fascists, Nazis, and Communists, the excavations for Peter's tomb and their results continued to be held in strict secrecy, and the presumed relics of Peter continued to rest in a box in Pius XII's apartment.

The Curse and the Flood — 1949

Since the early days of the basilica, writings claimed that a peculiar curse was associated with any attempt to excavate or disturb Peter's bones.[132] Every historical attempt to find Peter's relics had faced unexplainable and puzzling events. Pope Urban VIII, who had ordered the initial excavation for the Bernini baldacchino in the seventeenth century, himself fell ill, and many excavators at that time unexpectedly died while working in the Necropolis. Roman citizens (never passing on a good superstition) linked the proximity of these inexplicable events with a curse.[133]

The superstitious belief that a curse follows those who disturb graves is hardly a new one. The Roman belief in such a curse probably protected Peter's grave during the great early persecutions of Rome. Even the tombstone of the great William Shakespeare at Stratford-upon-Avon bears the inscription:

> Good friend, for Jesus' sake forbeare
>   To digg the dust enclosed heare;
> Bleste be the man that spares thes stones,
>   And curst be he that moves my bones.[134]

The line between archeologists and grave robbers is sometimes a narrow one. Many of the great tombs of history — for example, that of Genghis Khan — remain undiscovered or unopened partly because of fear or aversion. Most of those responsible for the excavation of Pharaoh Tutankhamen's tomb in the Valley of the Kings in Egypt in 1922 died remarkably quick deaths — attributed by the superstitious to the so-called Curse of Tut.

It was thus no surprise to superstitious workmen when disaster befell the Necropolis in 1949. During the fall of that year, immense rains inundated Italy and Rome. The Tiber rose to flood stage, but was still held within its banks by high stone embankments. In ancient times, before the embankments were built, Rome was regularly flooded by the Tiber. Now, suddenly and inexplicably, the Necropolis began to fill with water as if it alone, and not its surroundings, had returned to ancient times. Pumps were brought in, but could not keep up with the rising waters, which reached three to four feet deep in the Necropolis. It appeared the work of a decade and preserved antiquities of ancient Rome would be lost. Was it a special curse — St. Peter's curse? Finally, when all seemed hopeless, the collapse of an ancient pipe was discovered as the source of the flood.[135] With repairs, the water slowly receded and the Necropolis was saved, although not without damage. The secret excavations resumed, while the outside world remained completely oblivious to both the crisis and the excavations.

The Story Breaks — 1949

Beyond question, the excavators must have chafed at Pius's decade-long insistence on secrecy. Having discovered the great family tombs completely intact, and believing they had discovered Peter himself, they wanted fame and renown for their work.

The long wait ended on August 22, 1949, when an Italian journalist, Camille Gianfara (whose sources are still secret and unknown), published the story of the excavations.[136] The *New York Times* carried a front-page story headlined, "BONES OF ST. PETER FOUND."[137] The cover of *Time* magazine also proclaimed the discovery.

Over a year later, Pius XII broke his silence in a radio address. He affirmed that Peter's tomb had been found. He also indicated that human bones had been found, but needed additional testing. Shortly after his radio address in 1950, Pius invited George Strake and his family to Rome to celebrate the great success. The Strakes met in Rome with Montini, Kaas, McGeough, and others involved in the successful excavation. They met directly with Pius XII, who offered the Church's thanks for Strake's help. Ferrua and the excavators took bows for their accomplishments. George Strake was elated that his great project had been a wonderful success, validating his own beliefs and assisting the Church he so deeply loved. The Strakes believed the trip one of the great moments of their lives. Publicly, George Strake still kept his involvement wholly secret, and the Church, likewise, honored his anonymity.

Death of Walter Carroll

The Strakes were unable to meet with Walter Carroll — their friend and contact for the past decade. Earlier in 1950,

Carroll's great run as the genius behind impossible schemes had ended. As his biographer George Kemon wrote, he "lived to accomplish these tasks in pursuit of peace in Europe, and after the war was over, he laid down and died."[138] His brave heart, which had fought coronary illness since childhood, stopped in Washington, D.C.

Tributes flowed from all over the world: President Truman, General Mark Clark, Supreme Court Justice Robert Jackson (chief prosecutor at Nuremberg), and even an Italian prisoner at Dachau who recalled Carroll's timely, life-saving arrival there.[139] Montini and McGeough were deeply stricken by the loss of their great and brave friend. In September 1951, Montini and McGeough visited the United States.[140] Montini is quoted as telling Carroll's mother, "I have made a pilgrimage to the grave of my friend."[141] Together with McGeough he visited the Pittsburgh grave of their mutual friend, wartime comrade, and conspirator in a variety of concealed activities. Carroll's early death left a hole in Montini's heart. In later years, even as Pope Paul VI, he would on occasion visit with Carroll's brothers and no doubt express his sense of loss at brave Walter Carroll's premature death after surviving World War II.[142]

In the 1950s, George Strake, with other friends of Walter Carroll, financed the building of a large bell tower at Carroll's home church in Pittsburgh. Visitors today still describe the architecture of the bell tower and the church as stunning. The builders found it appropriate because Walter Carroll was a bell for decency and truth in an uncertain world. Now, with the bell ringing at dawn and dusk, they could look up and know he had gone to a wonderful place.

In 1951, Montini traveled across the United States by car, delighted to experience this strange country he had learned so much about from Carroll. Montini and Mc-

Geough drove all the way from Pittsburgh to Colorado to visit George Strake on his 1,200-acre estate at Glen Eyrie. For several days, they relived with the Strakes their wartime stories, spoke much of brave Walter Carroll and his schemes, and filled Strake in on the details of the apparently successful location of Peter's relics. They enjoyed together the magic of the Rockies, Queen's Canyon, Eagle Lake, and Glen Eyrie. The Strakes retain to this day the bed in which the future pope slept and occasionally offer the use of it to visitors.

The great mystery of Peter appeared solved. The story was closed — until a difficult and troublesome woman of great capability with an obsession for truth appeared on the scene. In reality, the greatest discoveries lay ahead — not behind. It would be Margherita Guarducci, not Ferrua and the excavators, who would make them.

CHAPTER FOURTEEN

MARGHERITA GUARDUCCI

Epigraphy is the study of ancient inscriptions. There are few more subtle and difficult subspecialties of archeology. The locations of the ancient inscriptions are often dark, unpleasant, and sometimes even dangerous. Epigraphers are a fountainhead of interesting stories often populated with bandits, snakes, scorpions, and tomb robbers pilfering ancient remains. In addition to the arduous nature of the work, this specialty requires fluency in the dead language involved, and often the ability to understand colloquialisms and rapidly evolving meanings from long-gone worlds. On rare occasions, it requires actually decrypting inscriptions made in long-ago codes. The epigraphist is the Sherlock Holmes of archeology, discovering truth by linking ancient signs one to another, many with meanings that were in use for only a few decades.

Twentieth-century Italy was profoundly sexist. The Italian female stereotype of a mother cooking pasta was, in fact, not an atypical view held in that place and age. Margherita Guarducci profoundly broke the mold. By all descriptions, she could be considered an early Italian feminist, accomplishing amazing archeological breakthroughs in a time and profession dominated by men. She was deeply in love with men — but they were men who had died thousands of years before her birth. She had little use for the men or world of her time. While existing in the present, she lived in the past.

The great archeologists of fiction are invariably sophisticated men of great panache and impressive physical ability and appearance. Indiana Jones of *Raiders of the Lost Ark* battles natives, snakes, and Nazis with skill and aplomb. Professor Robert Langdon of *The Da Vinci Code* rushes through a variety of ancient sites adroitly avoiding a variety of deadly conspirators, accompanied by the beautiful Sophie Neveu. It is sometimes said that truth is stranger than fiction, because fiction must be written to seem possible. No writer of fiction could have invented Margherita Guarducci. The brilliant, real-life archeological genius Guarducci, whose discoveries would rival or exceed those of any fictional rivals, was a short, thin, frail-looking woman, whose uninspiring presence concealed an unconquerable spirit, intense energy, and a mind of utter genius. She was truly "a diamond bit" seeking the truth. Before her long life ended, she would perform mental feats, find archeological wonders, and fight battles at least as great as her counterparts in fiction.

She was born in Florence in 1902, to a family of ancient roots. Her long life began shortly after the new century opened. It would end only as the twentieth century closed. It was an amazing journey. Guarducci graduated in 1924 with a degree in archeology from the University of Bologna. She then attended courses and began her life's work at the National School of Archeology in Rome and the Italian Archaeological School of Athens.[143] Almost immediately, she was recognized by her teachers as a rare genius in early Greek epigraphy and became the leading accomplice of Federico Halbherr, a famous archeologist.[144] Guarducci had a fanatical capacity for frenzied work — often under difficult conditions. It was her "firm, but gentle character" that defined Guarducci.[145] She was rigidly scientific, and, once convinced of the truth, totally unbending in her beliefs.

She had the active, bright eyes of a bird, accompanied by a constant half-smile. A string of pearls always adorned her neck, and bobby pins maintained her perpetual bun. From the beginning to the end of her long life, she retained the same string and the same half-smile. Guarducci was a great speaker and teacher with an astounding memory, who could recite verbatim many long, ancient Greek and Minoan texts, sometimes unconsciously moving her hands to demonstrate the actual inscriptions she had found. Once launched upon a problem, she would devote years or even decades and tireless energy to the hunt for truth, often under terrible conditions. In an age of male supremacy, and in an Italy famous for sexism and corruption, she conceded nothing on account of position, influence, or male dominance. Her friend, patron, and companion was the truth.

Guarducci's world was the Greek, Minoan, and Roman world of 3,000 B.C.–A.D. 500. Her constant half-smile reflected the amusement of a time traveler from a long-ago world at the folly of the present world to which she had somehow been transported. One acquaintance compared her, perhaps appropriately, to Savonarola, a Dominican friar burned at the stake in Guarducci's native Florence in 1498 for speaking unwanted truths. But the same acquaintance also compared Guarducci to Catherine of Siena, a fearless truth-teller, among the greatest of medieval saints.[146] Indeed, traits of both Savonarola and Catherine were present in Guarducci.

It is impossible to understand Guarducci without understanding her Florentine roots. She grew up in the Florence of the Uffizi Gallery with Botticelli, Titian, Giotto, and Leonardo. Even today, much of Florence remains frozen in the Renaissance of the fourteenth to seventeenth centuries. The city's great age was fueled by the rediscovery of ancient civilizations. To walk around old Florence is to time travel to the world of the Medici and Donatello, of Michelangelo, and through them even further back to the great classical ages of ancient Greece and Rome. Guarducci's world consisted of the Renaissance palaces, Ponte Vecchio, Michelangelo's *David*, and the Fountain of Neptune in the Piazza della Signoria. She gazed and wondered at Brunelleschi's great dome of Santa Maria del Fiore and at Giotto's works. She was not a child of the twentieth century. From childhood, her world was a world of long ago — her loves and dreams were things and people long gone and untainted by the shabby, mercantile twentieth century. She could gaze upon Michelangelo's *David* and through it see the *Hermes* of Praxiteles or even the lost sculptures of Phidias.

It is also impossible to understand Guarducci without understanding the age of archeology when she entered the profession. It was not the dawn of archeology, but it was the morning of that science as a science. Discoverers like Battista Beldoni in Egypt and Heinrich Schliemann of Troy/Mycenae (modern-day Mykonos) fame had popularized the study, but they were as much adventurers as scientists. Their methods were often crude and unscientific, designed to discover wonderful artifacts as treasure hunters and bring them back to great museums like the Pergamon in Berlin and the British Museum in London. They were much less concerned with systematically studying and preserving sites. Kenneth Harl wrote cruelly, but accurately, of the great

Schliemann that he had done to the Trojans what the Greeks could not do: destroy their entire city.[147] In the 1920s, science began to replace the treasure hunt for artifacts. Archeologists started using a grid system, accurately surveying and carefully studying, strata by strata, to establish chronological order and gain all the information actually available from an ancient site. Epigraphy, photography, forensic evidence, and, much later, carbon dating and various tools of remote survey became implements of a much more scientific and thorough archeology. Guarducci was deeply committed to the use of these scientific methods and tools to arrive at the truth. Like other well-trained archeologists of the period, she was horrified at the destructive treasure hunts of earlier archeological investigations. She viewed herself as a scientist committed to finding scientific truth.

Guarducci's Early Career

She made her name in Cretan excavations and epigraphy. The city of Gortyna in Crete is one of the oldest continuously occupied cities in the world, dating back some six thousand years to the late neolithic period. In 1884, Federico Halbherr with others found more than ten meters of a circular stone wall inscribed by sculptors between 525 and 450 B.C. with what came to be known as the "queen of inscriptions," or the Gortyna Code. For nearly forty years, the massive inscription — clearly a legal code from the city just prior to the Golden Age of Greece — remained largely unintelligible to the world. Halbherr's career, while epic, was much more Indiana Jones than careful study, and he had heard of Guarducci's genius — she was already widely known to be a rare talent in epigraphy. Halbherr associated Guarducci in his work and became her mentor by 1929. For many years, and after Halbherr's death, Guarducci worked on decrypting the massive legal code. She succeeded, and "the great inscription," as it came to be known, provided the fullest available picture of how the Greeks actually regulated their lives on the edge of the Golden Age. The inscription covered subjects such as adultery (a small fine), rape (a big fine), divorce, inheritance rights, crime, arrests, and suits. Changes made over the seventy-five-year period of the code reflected it being amended to increase the rights of slaves and decrease the rights of women. Guarducci then proceeded to systematically record and translate into Latin (in those days the official language of archeology) thousands of Cretan inscriptions covering many hundreds of years. Over a twenty-year period, she published these in a multivolume series called *Inscriptiones Creticae*, in her name and the name of her beloved, deceased mentor. Guarducci's work was not simply famous; it was foundational. Her genius, combined with more than twenty years of tedious study, provided the most complete view of the actual life of a Greek city-state on the very cusp of the Golden Age. In addition, she opened inscriptions dating back to legendary Minoan days, bringing them to the modern world for the first time. She was universally hailed as one of archeology's great geniuses.

Against all odds in an age and profession still dominated by men, Guarducci became, through sheer genius, a famous archeologist, a much-published author, and a professor of epigraphy at the University of Rome, one of the largest and oldest universities in the world.[148] She was notorious for lack of tact or political skill. Abrupt and lacking relationship to modern people or institutions, Guarducci accomplished everything through raw brilliance. Paraphrasing the famous Italian antiquarian Federico Zeri, she had no clients or ideology other than the truth.

Arthur Schopenhauer wrote, "Genius hits a target no one else can see." For this reason, genius is both a blessing and a curse. It excites at least as much resentment and envy as appreciation. Thus Vincent Van Gogh, regarded as a bizarre failure, did not sell a single painting during his lifetime. Nikola Tesla died broke and alone in a hotel room, regarded by many as a fraud. Resentment and envy seem to build to particularly great heights when the genius is a woman surrounded by men of inferior talent. If the legends are true, this goes back to ancient times and Cassandra, whose genius was seeing the future, ignored by everyone when she famously warned her fellow Trojans to beware Greeks bearing gifts. Or consider Saint Joan of Arc, the greatest female military leader of all time, burned as a witch by men who could not conceive that a mere woman could possess such genius and, therefore, believed the devil must be aiding her. Guarducci's genius unveiled would in short order prove both a gift and a curse, exciting some of the same sort of envy and disbelief as Cassandra and Joan of Arc faced.

Guarducci in the Necropolis

In April 1952, Ludwig Kaas died. In a mark of affection and respect, Pius caused Kaas to be buried in the Necropolis close to the location where they believed Peter had been found. The excavation team had lost its leader, although Ferrua and the other excavators had kept him practically shut out of the day-to-day proceedings in the work.

By May 1952, the presumed bones of Peter continued to rest in the pope's apartments, where they had remained for a decade. Ferrua and the excavators had reported to Pius XII that, other than the presumed bones and the later altars erected by Constantine and others, few references to Peter could be located. They found numerous inscriptions, but they considered these unintelligible and meaningless graffiti. The Ferrua team was celebrated in a *Time* magazine cover story in March 1950 as archeological geniuses and pioneers.

In that year, the world of the Ferrua team would begin to turn upside down. Montini, a friend of Guarducci's ancient Florentine family, extended an invitation to her to be one of the first non-Vatican employees to tour the excavation. It is probable that Montini and Strake discussed the necessity of bringing in outside experts at substantial cost during Montini's Glen Eyrie visit. Like Ludwig Kaas, Montini was uncomfortable with the work of the Ferrua team. He personally invited Guarducci to study the Necropolis, likely envisioning she would be there for a week or so. That week became decades.

Guarducci entered the Necropolis and was immediately horrified by the team's evident failure to follow basic archeological procedures.[149] It was apparent that this was one of the world's greatest archeological sites, and it had been badly mistreated. Many inscriptions, some painted, had been uncovered and then left without protection in the moist, destructive underworld for a decade. History was literally vanishing. Astonishingly, no systematic photographic record had been made. When Guarducci saw the Graffiti Wall, it was apparent to her trained eye that the peculiar scratches were not meaningless, as Ferrua reported, but rather had very special meanings.[150] Finally, in a tomb thirty feet from the center of the altar constructed by Constantine, she found an overlooked inscription meaning "Christian men buried near your body."[151] She made a full report to Montini and Pius. Following this report, and in the wake of Ludwig Kaas's death, Pius made the surprising decision to replace Kaas not with Ferrua, but with Margherita Guarducci. In 1953, Guarducci was made head of the excavations. Kirschbaum and Ferrua were abruptly excluded from further leadership in the Necropolis (although they retained administrative positions at the Vatican).[152]

Given Guarducci's typical lack of tact, it is hardly surprising that Ferrua was furious. He viewed Guarducci as an incompetent interloper preying on the glory of his work. Under the best circumstances, a laywoman superseding and criticizing a priest would not be calculated to build close friendship. Guarducci's abruptness inspired deep, long-lasting resentment in Ferrua.

Things got worse when Guarducci noticed a photograph of an inscription on a wall in a 1951 article by Ferrua. When she searched for the inscription at its site, it was no longer in the Necropolis. She learned that Ferrua had removed it to his home, ostensibly to study it.[153] A direct order from Pius XII secured its return.[154] This critical inscription — without which the mystery would perhaps have remained unsolved — read, "Peter is here."[155] It was originally located on the Graffiti Wall a few feet from the Trophy of Gaius at the center of the Vatican.

Ferrua no doubt regarded the conflict over this critical, removed inscription as an attack, not only on his competence, but on his honor. In his view, Guarducci was an incompetent poacher — a pilot fish who had come to steal credit for his work by telling Pius and Montini whatever they wanted to hear. Over time, the interaction between the two deteriorated, with a bitterly resentful Ferrua targeting Guarducci's work. Indeed, he seems to have developed an insatiable hatred for Guarducci. Ferrua would denounce her work as "fundamentally wrong" and use a combination of invective and humor to make fun of her.[156] In contrast, Guarducci seems largely to have ignored Ferrua. This adversarial relationship would launch one of the greatest and bitterest controversies in archeological history.[157]

While Ferrua retained various executive positions as a Vatican antiquities functionary, he was barred from further leadership in the excavation for the remainder of Pius XII's life. Ferrua would, nevertheless, slowly climb to the top of the Vatican antiquities structure.

Shortly after taking charge of the excavation, Guarducci noticed a hole in the bottom of the Graffiti Wall very close to the Trophy of Gaius. When she examined it, she found that it was an ancient, marble-lined wall niche. She asked a workman, Giovanni Segoni, whether any artifact or relic had been found there. Segoni said that, in fact, bones had been discovered in the cavity eleven years earlier in 1942.[158] Kaas, horrified by Ferrua's disrespect for remains, had asked Segoni to remove the bones from the marble niche, place them in a wooden box, and label and place the box in a storeroom where they had lain for more than a decade, totally forgotten.[159] Like the fictional storage of the Ark of the Covenant in *Raiders of the Lost Ark*, Guarducci had stumbled upon the solution to the mystery of Peter, but it would be many years before she or anyone else realized it. These bones seemed irrelevant given Ferrua's discovery of the assumed bones of Peter under the Trophy of Gaius. So Guarducci stored the Graffiti Wall bones again in the storeroom, resolving to have them forensically examined. Meanwhile, the presumed bones of Peter remained in the papal apartment.

Guarducci's first task in light of the decade-old deterioration of the uncovered epigraphs was to photograph everything. Strake continued to finance her extensive activity. She approached the task of learning the truth with fanatical devotion — spending every morning in the grey necropolis examining the inscriptions, and poring over piles of photographs every evening. Other than her teaching at the university, work surrounding the secret excavation beneath the Vatican became her entire life.

The Graffiti Wall inscriptions were a "forest" of scratches, interlineated one on top of another or densely packed. Her first job was to separate the individual "trees" from the forest — that is, to separate for individual examination the inscriptions one by one as they were actually made. Using photography, magnification, and physical inspection over many months, she tenaciously did exactly that, separating individual inscriptions into those made at one time with one pair of hands so long ago. She then proceeded to decode the hundreds of inscriptions she found. It was a task akin to separating a massive pile of pickup sticks without destroying any of them.

The Necropolis had originally been sealed by the construction of the first St. Peter's Basilica in 337, so it was apparent that all inscriptions must predate that. Her first great find was the faded inscription, "*In Hoc Vince*" — translated, "In This Conquer."[160] This inscription must have been carved less than eighteen years after Constantine's victory. It confirmed to Guarducci the story that Constantine and his troops claimed to have seen these words written in the sky with a cross the day before their epic victory at the Milvian Bridge. This fantastic account had come to be widely regarded as a myth invented much later. Yet Guarducci's discovery provided incontrovertible confirmation that this story had begun to circulate while the witnesses were still alive — it was not a later fabrication.

Chapter Fifteen

The Inscriptions Speak

From 1953 to 1958, Guarducci focused her attention on studying the inscriptions on the Graffiti Wall and the adjacent Red Wall. In the dark Necropolis, she would study the inscriptions by flashlight. On occasion in the half-light, she would close her eyes and draw them with her hands, as the ancient Christians had, in an effort to understand their meaning. Sometimes she would even feel the stones themselves, as if seeking a spiritual unity with the authors. Ferrua had reported the inscriptions to be meaningless or unintelligible graffiti. Guarducci, after unflagging study day and night for five years, uncovered profound meaning.

Guarducci's task resembled the most famous of all feats of epigraphy — the discovery and use of the Rosetta Stone. Ancient Egyptian hieroglyphs were idea symbols later replaced by phonetic symbols linked to spoken words. The hieroglyphs became a dead language: still present throughout Egypt, but unreadable to anyone. In 1796, the Rosetta Stone was discovered. It contained substantially identical texts of the same decree in hieroglyphs, Greek, and Egyptian, providing the key to unlocking the forgotten language.

For Guarducci, the key to unlock the meaning of the inscriptions in the Necropolis was an understanding of the early Christians, their faith, and the danger surrounding them. Symbols such as a "P" surrounded by keys would be meaningless to a non-Christian, but a Christian would see this and recall Christ's words to Peter: "I will give you the keys to the kingdom of heaven" (Mt 16:19). Likewise, the Alpha and Omega symbols (the beginning and the end of the Greek alphabet) would appear as meaningless prattle to non-Christians, but they held significant meaning to Christians, for whom Christ is the Alpha and Omega.[161] An "R" symbol with a line to a "T" (also used as a cross symbol) would have had no meaning to a non-Christian Roman but profound meaning to an early Christian, to whom it represented resurrection for all, purchased by Christ's death. To understand these inscriptions, it was essential to view them through the lens of ancient Christian belief. These were phonetic symbols used not simply for sounds, but also for complex ideas.

In the gulags of the Soviet Union as early as the 1920s, prisoners from the White Sea prison camps developed a nearly universal "top code," allowing them to communicate with each other by sounds not understandable to their guards. In much the same way, and for the same reasons, early Christians developed their own code of inscriptions, understandable to each other, but not to the Roman authorities.

Guarducci broke this code.[162]

Various Greek letters were used as symbols for spiritual concepts. The Alpha and Omega symbols, for example, signified the beginning and end. A Christ symbol (Chi-Rho) followed by Alpha and Omega expressed the thought that Christ was the beginning and the end. A name followed by Omega and Alpha meant that someone's life had ended, but their real life with Christ in heaven had just begun.[163] Similarly, Guarducci found a whole range of letters representing spiritual realities, such as "R" for resurrection, "M" or "MA" for Mary, and "T" for the cross. Further, she realized lines were used to connect spiritual meanings with names — for example, the Christ symbol connected by a line to an "R" (for resurrection) and a "T" (for the cross), connected by another line to a "V" (for victory).[164]

The Christians also communicated in abbreviations because of their medium: scratches on rock, made quickly to avoid detection. Think of the difference between communicating through tweets or texts today and the full sentence structure found in books. Current acronyms used as shorthand in social media, such as "LOL" or "OMG," while not comparable in substance, could arguably be comparable in abbreviation to these early Christian graffiti.

Guarducci examined Christian inscriptions across the area that comprised the ancient Roman Empire — particularly in Asia Minor and in Rome. These proved that the code was not random. The inscriptions had been used over and over again by Christians at many early sites and possessed established, well understood meanings. Guarducci's encyclopedic survey of several hundred years of Christian epigraphs proved that the Christians were indeed speaking to each other in coded language unknown to anyone who did not understand their faith. To draw another modern comparison, these Christian inscriptions from the first through fourth centuries would be the equivalent of Capitalist graffiti on Lenin's tomb during the Cold War.

The clear heroism and deep faith and courage of these early Christians in the heart of the Roman capital deeply affected Guarducci. They were to her a voice from two thousand years ago commanding the "greatest attention."[165] As she wrote:

> In studying the problem of St. Peter's tomb, we find a third voice, that of the epigraphs, joining in the eloquent testimony of ancient authors and excavations. It is a voice that we must hear with the greatest attention, since the epigraphs are usually precious witnesses bringing us the direct, live echo of past events.[166]

She had to travel back to her own early Christian roots to recall the early teachings that provided the code to unlock the inscriptions. In the words of an old English song, once she was blind, but now she could see. Over time the inscriptions deeply changed Guarducci herself. Virtually all of her work prior to the inscriptions had been done in Crete and preclassical and classical Greece. Her physical work with these ancient Christian inscriptions, coupled with her realization of the deep and genuine faith of the early believers, seems to have greatly deepened Guarducci's own faith.

The theological implications of the Graffiti Wall are still profound and moving today. The inscriptions highlight the continuity of Christian belief down through the millennia. Peter occupied a central role in the Church and in the hearts of the early believers. Early Christians prayed to Christ and also invoked the aid of Mary, Peter, and other saints. From earliest times, Christians believed in eternal life unlocked by Christ's death upon the Cross. These ancient inscriptions made clear that Christianity was not simply an evolving cult. As early as 250–300, Christians believed in the same basic tenets we accept today, and people were willing to risk their lives to create the inscriptions that expressed these beliefs.

The Graffiti Wall stood next to the Red Wall, where the bones presumed to be those of Peter had been found years before. The Red Wall was built of bricks containing seals dated to A.D. 160. It had been partly covered in 250 by the Graffiti Wall.[167] Guarducci first found within the Graffiti Wall the tantalizing inscription, "Near Peter."[168] Then, Guarducci made an explosive discovery. Placing the inscription recovered from Ferrua's house in its proper place on the Graffiti Wall, she read, "Peter is within."[169] Near the Red Wall, Guarducci found even earlier Christian inscriptions such as the familiar Christian fish symbol dating from the early 100s. She also found inscriptions such as, "Peter, pray for me" inscribed in the late 100s. Over and over, she deciphered references to Peter on the Graffiti Wall — in the end, she found his name inscribed there more than twenty times.[170] This could not be a coincidence. Clearly early Christians had prayed to Peter here, in the presence of his actual relics. In fact, the Graffiti Wall bearing these repeated inscriptions to Peter seemed very much like an ancient tombstone marking his final resting place.

She did not realize it yet, but after five long years, Guarducci had found the clues that would eventually solve the mystery.

CHAPTER SIXTEEN

THE BONES SPEAK

In 1956, Pope Pius XII brought in Professor Venerando Correnti of Palermo University, perhaps Europe's greatest medical anthropologist, to make a detailed clinical study of the presumed bones of Saint Peter, unearthed more than thirteen years before by Ferrua and Kirschbaum. Since their initial examination by the general practitioner in 1942, the bones had remained stored in the pope's quarters, untouched and unquestioned. Kirschbaum had written that it was "irresistible" that these were Peter's bones. The excavators believed and reported that they had found Peter.[171]

As it turned out, the original team of excavators had been very wrong. Professor Correnti soon discovered that the bones were from several individuals, not one.[172] In addition, they included fragments of bones from animals. Before his death in 1958, Pius XII was informed that the bones were not Peter's. Although we have no direct record of his reaction, Pius was surely bitterly disappointed. The Apostle Project launched under his direction twenty years before had uncovered unbelievable Roman archeological ruins and strong evidence of Peter's presence and death in Rome — but it had not uncovered Peter's relics, the incontrovertible evidence the pope had most hoped for. Nor did Pius apparently know the extent of Guarducci's ongoing investigation of the inscriptions. Sadly, Pius died with his dreams for the Apostle Project still not entirely fulfilled.

The quest continued, however, even after the pope's death. By 1960, Correnti had completed his examination of the bones that had so long been presumed to be Peter's. He concluded that the bones were in fact those of two men too young to be Peter and an old woman.[173] Kirschbaum and Ferrua were stunned and angered by the results, which they refused to believe.

Guarducci remembered the bones that had been discovered in the Graffiti Wall and saved by Kaas in 1942. The inscription "Peter is within" from that wall could very well have applied to those bones, along with the many coded references to Peter she had found on the Graffiti Wall. Perhaps the Graffiti Wall inscriptions had been the ancient Christians' way of secretly marking the shrine and offering prayers there. If that were the case, the Graffiti Wall would in fact be an ancient tombstone. Guarducci presented the Graffiti Wall bones to Correnti for examination in 1962. They had remained in storage for twenty years, taken out only once in 1953 when Guarducci learned of their existence and briefly examined them.

Correnti's Exam

In those twenty years in storage, it appeared a mouse had crawled into the box and died — its full skeleton remained intact.[174] Correnti also found small fragments of animal bones and unrelated human bone fragments, which was to be expected since (long before the Family Tombs) Vatican Hill had been used as a body dump for thousands of years before Peter's death. But Correnti also found several remains of a single person. Extensive forensics were possible since pieces of cranium, jaw, a tooth, vertebrae, pelvis, legs, arms, and hands were all present.[175] What Correnti found when examining the Graffiti Wall bones was astonishing. The bones, found very close to the inscription "Peter is here," were determined to be those of a sixty- to seventy-year-old robust male, approximately Peter's supposed age when he died.[176] Even more amazing, the bones had originally been buried in the dirt next to the Graffiti Wall under the Trophy of Gaius rather than in the wall, as evidenced by soil still adhering to them after 1,700 years. It was also determined that they had once been covered with an early purple and gold cloth whose dye was of a type only used by Imperial Romans of the first to third centuries.[177] Amazingly, the bones were also compatible with the remains of a person crucified upside down. The feet had been viciously cut off as the Romans were wont to do when removing a crucified corpse, because it was easier than removing nails.[178] The bones had been moved to the Graffiti Wall niche from the dirt under Gaius's Trophy between 250, when the Graffiti Wall was built, and 337 when the Necropolis was sealed.

In 1963, Cardinal Montini (who as a monsignor in 1939 had dispatched Father Carroll on the mission to George Strake, and had retained Guarducci in 1952) succeeded Pope Saint John XXIII, taking the name Paul VI. Guarducci met with the new pope to share the astounding results of the examination of the Graffiti Wall bones.[179] The pope cautiously authorized various additional tests by Correnti. These tests proved the purple cloth adhering to the bones to be of Imperial Roman, second- or third-century origin, both by their weave and their dye. Moreover, the dirt fragments on the bones matched exactly the soil in the central grave under the Trophy of Gaius.[180] Additional forensic examinations validated Correnti's conclusions.

When presented with the results, Ferrua completely denied their validity.

In late 1964, Guarducci compiled a report for publication by the Vatican. The report concluded that it was virtually certain that Peter's bones had been found. It further deduced that Peter had originally been buried in the soil at the center of St. Peter's, marked by Gaius's Trophy. His remains were then covered with a purple cloth and removed (between 250 when the Graffiti Wall was built and 337 when St. Peter's was completed) to the small, marble-lined Graffiti Wall niche marked with the encoded epigraphs.[181] They had remained there until 1941, since the niche walls were totally intact. At least twenty inscriptions on the wall referred to Peter and had clearly been written there before the sealing of the Necropolis in 337. Paul VI submitted the report and all working materials to five disinterested experts — three archeologists and two specialists in Greek epigraphy. All five concluded unanimously that the report was impeccably accurate and that Guarducci had found Peter.[182]

Ferrua's reaction was that the pope was simply "deaf" to information and that Guarducci was a woman whose "faith" caused her to overstate or misinterpret results.[183]

Chapter Seventeen

Ferrua's Revenge

The publication of Guarducci's report in February 1965 initiated one of the greatest firestorms of controversy in archeological history.[184] The critics were led, not surprisingly, by Antonio Ferrua.[185]

He attacked Guarducci's earlier book on the inscriptions as the product of an authoress "with faith that ought to move mountains," but who was "fundamentally wrong."[186] She was portrayed as doctoring her results to support her faith — a curious inversion of the facts, since it seems her faith had come alive as a result of the inscriptions. She was ridiculed for identifying the remains of the mouse that had crawled into the storage box and died as the relics of Peter. Further, Ferrua pointed to two coins found nearby, one dating from A.D. 357, the other from the Middle Ages. Ferrua relied on this as proof that the bones could not possibly date as early as Guarducci supposed. He also submitted a report to Pope Paul VI ridiculing Guarducci's claims and pleading with the pope to ignore them as wholly speculative and only a woman's act of faith.[187]

Reading the attacks, it is hard to ignore Ferrua's repeated reference to Guarducci as "a woman" operating only on unsupported faith. Perhaps this is simply an example of the endemic sexism of mid-twentieth-century Italy, but coming from a priest it certainly gives one pause. After all, Christ's first chosen messenger was a woman — the Samaritan Woman at the well in the fourth chapter of the Gospel according to John. This woman had been married five times and was living unmarried with a sixth man, yet Christ chose her as his first messenger to the Samaritans. Many early Christian inscriptions depicted her with her jar, including inscriptions in the Necropolis. What's more, given the scientific investigation and mountain of evidence assembled by Guarducci, Correnti, and the team of five experts, it seems like willful blindness on the part of Ferrua to dismiss the results as simply an act of Guarducci's faith.

Guarducci, who had already spent nearly fifteen years on the Apostle Project, worked for almost three more years to answer Ferrua and other critics with additional scientific and forensic studies. Examination of the purple and gold threads by chemists at the University of Rome proved once again that they were textiles from the first through the third centuries. The weave and purple dye had been used only by Imperial Romans of the period. It was also determined that the later coins and many others left by Christians had fallen through cracks in the walls over the millennia, particularly since a coin was found in the Graffiti Wall dating from A.D. 14 — *before* the Graffiti Wall was even framed. The Graffiti Wall niche, where the bones had initially been found, was dismantled by experts. Bricks of Roman origin proved the niche and the bones had remained untouched since original construction — certainly before the construction of the first basilica circa 337.

In 1966, Guarducci responded to her critics by pamphlet and article. In her view, overwhelming cumulative evidence proved that these bones, located only two feet from the center of the Necropolis and surrounded by at least twenty inscriptions predating 337 indicating "near Peter," "Peter is here," and the like, belonged to Peter.[188] She asserted they were buried originally in the soil under the Trophy of Gaius, then moved between 250 and 337 into the concealment of the Graffiti Wall. She believed it likely that the bones had been moved to protect them during the construction of the original St. Peter's Basilica.[189]

Ferrua organized a furious resistance by numerous Vatican insiders, begging the pope to ignore the bones. He argued there was no real evidence that Peter's body was ever buried on the hill as opposed to thrown in the Tiber. Ferrua later described Paul VI as simply "deaf" like Pius XII.[190]

On June 26, 1968, Pope Paul VI announced to the world that Peter's bones had been found, concluding that the bone fragments recovered by Guarducci from the Necropolis had been identified "in a way that we can consider convincing."[191] The following day, the bones were returned in fiberglass boxes to the Graffiti Wall niche from which they had emerged more than twenty-five years before. The largest of them remained visible in the wall through transparent fiberglass.

But in the Vatican that day there remained at least one who rejected and bitterly resented these findings — Guarducci's archnemesis, Antonio Ferrua.[192] Following his exclusion from active participation in the excavation after Guarducci was placed in charge,[193] he continued to hold a variety of powerful positions within the Vatican. By the late 1970s, he had been made head of the Commission on Archeology — and he waited.

Requiescat in Pace

Pope Pius XII died in 1958. Fittingly, George Strake established the Pius XII Memorial Library at St. Louis University, leading a fund drive to endow it with $5 million to micro-film and thereby preserve all of the ancient documents of the Vatican library in Rome that had provided the clues guiding the Peter excavation. Strake wanted to preserve these invaluable documents. As happened in the catastrophic destruction of the ancient libraries at Alexandria and Constantinople, a single fire, bomb, or modern vandal could have destroyed the only copies of the vast array of ancient documents housed within the Vatican Library. The work involved the filming of well over a million books and manuscripts, and more than thirty-seven thousand ancient codices, some crumbling.

In the 1950s, Strake also gave away his beloved Glen Eyrie, selling it for a nominal price to a Protestant organization associated with Billy Graham's message. The buyers also sought to acquire Strake's legendary acreage at nearby Eagle Lake, but he refused to include it. He simply couldn't bring himself to part with it. On the day of closing, however, Strake said he had prayed about it all night and threw in his beloved Eagle Lake property for nothing. This generous act was consistent with a life spent sacrificially giving away even the things he treasured most.

In 1969, Strake died suddenly, at the age of seventy-four. On August 6, his car stopped while he was on a drive near Columbus, Texas.[194] He climbed out and began to push it in the hot August sun. The task was too much — his great heart stopped. He did not reach his objective of giving away his last dollar with his last breath, but he made a strong attempt. He left almost all of his remaining assets to a foundation to continue his work. Friends mourned him from Texas to Rome, including his friend, Pope Paul VI. His financing of the Apostle Project remained secret, even at his funeral and in his obituary. But Strake died secure in the knowledge that Peter had been located.

Within a short time, another great tree fell — Archbishop Joseph McGeough. Following his involvement in the Apostle Project and in the various events of World War II, Paul VI sent him as a special emissary to South Africa to oppose apartheid, and then on a final, unsuccessful mission to Ireland to end its religious conflicts.

These deaths were a blow to Guarducci, whose friends and defenders were slowly vanishing. Only Paul VI himself remained to maintain her position in the Vatican.

Ferrua meanwhile continued his campaign against Guarducci and her discoveries. In reviews, which he wrote directly or inspired, Ferrua questioned Guarducci, her findings and, specifically, the authentication of the Graffiti Wall bones now on display in the Necropolis as those of Saint Peter. Over time, Ferrua slowly became the most powerful Vatican official in archeology, gaining control of the vast Necropolis.

In December 1971, *National Geographic* published an article describing Guarducci's great discovery and featuring her as central to the excavation project. Ferrua was mentioned only as an unnamed scientist who questioned the discovery.[195]

In 1977, the Vatican published a small book by Guarducci, *Peter: The Rock on Which the Church Is Built*, beginning with Paul VI's thanks for the successful discovery of Peter's relics. Clearly, Guarducci's great work was held in great esteem by those at the highest levels of the Catholic Church. But very soon the tide would turn.

Chapter Eighteen

The Necropolis Uncovered

Margherita Guarducci focused her greatest efforts from 1952 forward on locating Peter and decoding the inscriptions. However, she likewise expended great energy in preserving, studying, and understanding the underground Necropolis. The area was in substantial disrepair when she arrived, and it was part of Guarducci's genius to recognize the treasures the Necropolis held for archeologists. It contained the ashes, bones, and memorials of more than one thousand Romans from the height of Roman power, dating mostly from A.D. 160 to 250. It was in effect a village of more than twenty-two major family tombs built along a road more than one hundred feet long on the side of Vatican Hill. Before they were covered by the original basilica, the tombs had overlooked a large highway leading into Rome.

   Such tombs had been constructed for two principal reasons: to display the importance of the involved family to the world and to provide a meeting place for the family itself to hold parties and remember the dead. On the Feast of Parentalia (similar to the Mexican Day of the Dead) and at other times, families would gather to feast in the tombs, often dining on flat sarcophagus lids set up as dining room tables "to pass the evening with pleasant talk."[196] The excavation team had identified the tombs by letters — "A" built first and then succeeding letters. Most held single families, but some were more like early condominiums, used and owned by several families.

When she was placed in charge of the excavation, Guarducci invited some of the greatest experts of the age to explore and detail the tombs, including Jocelyn Toynbee and a bevy of famous British and German archeologists. The earlier secrecy disappeared, and a large international effort to study the tombs ensued.

A certain haunting tragedy filled the site. Once magnificent structures high on a hill overlooking Eternal Rome in its greatest age now lay long abandoned, fifteen to sixty feet underground. The Roman Empire itself was long gone, but the art and sculpture within the tombs was breathtaking. The famous tomb of the chariot features a magnificent mosaic floor depicting a long-ago rider and chariot. The tomb of the Julii was almost schizophrenic, combining pagan and Christian murals, mixing Jonah and the Good Shepherd with Christ depicted as the pagan god Helios. So-called Tomb "F," built for freed slaves, was an extraordinary kaleidoscope of bright and vivid murals, ranging from swans swimming forever in an idyllic landscape to flowered candelabras with blue blooms, to a unique early *trompe l'oeil* mask appearing to hang from a wall. In another mural, Venus reclines on a mussel shell carried by Tritons, anticipating Titian's *Venus of Urbino* in Florence, while nearby huntsmen forever pursue lions. Indeed, many of the tomb paintings foreshadow the themes of the Renaissance, and their children may be found in museums from the Louvre to the Uffizi. Two tombs in particular tell stories — one happy and one sad.

The Tomb of the Marcii

This was the massive tomb of a rich and apparently jolly ex-slave named Quintus Marcius Hermes. The Marcii prospered in Rome despite their lowly beginnings. Their impressive tomb is the third largest in the Necropolis and faces south, where it once overlooked the road before its burial beneath Constantine's basilica. Its reddish brown brick exteriors once proudly proclaimed the wealth of the Marcii, but it is the interior that truly reveals their story.[197]

In addition to grand scenes of blue skies and rivers with ducks, red fish, and white flamingos, and the sea with dolphins, mythical sea horses, and seals, the tomb contains a set of scenes resembling movie posters in a modern theater.[198]

To adorn their final resting place, the Marcii picked two extraordinary scenes from Euripides. Euripides could be called the Steven Spielberg of ancient Greece. He authored approximately ninety-two plays, of which perhaps eighteen survive. He was most famous as the first playwright to humanize his characters so that even today an audience can identify with them as people. In the tomb, one scene, from *The Bacchae*, depicts a king named Pentheus being stabbed and killed by his own mother, driven mad by the gods. The second, from *Alcestis*, portrays the hero Hercules rescuing the Princess Alcestis from the depths of Hades itself, restoring her to her husband and life. It is obviously a hopeful scene for a tomb, although there is no record that the Marcii were so fortunate. In addition to the Euripides scenes, the Marcii included paintings of the mother of Rome's founders and a mural of Leda and the Swan.

The tomb is surprisingly cheerful, and the centerpiece is the Sarcophagus of Quintus himself and his wife

Marcia — their portraits joined by an inscription proclaiming their eternal love for one another.

The Tomb of the Valerii

There is no sadder place in the Necropolis than the tomb of the Valerii. It is the largest of all the tombs, built around A.D. 160 at the height of the Pax Romana and Roman power.[199] It is massively and ornately decorated with images of gods (like Oceanus and Pan) and philosophers. The tomb is commanded by a striking bust of an intensely proud, bearded family founder, Gaius Valerius Hermes. Nearby is the bust of his wife, Flavia, chin in hand, pensively staring into eternity. Likewise, there is a portrait of his daughter and a cheerful-looking bust of his four-year-old grandson, Gaius, contemplating with hope a future that would never come.

Inscriptions within this sad place make clear that Gaius's daughter, grandson, and wife all died before him, leaving him stripped of his family. Finally, the tomb contained two death masks, each made at the time of death. The first is of young Gaius, no longer the plump, bubbling child of the bust, but instead with a face tortured by illness and eyes forever closed. The second is the death mask of Gaius himself, thin, sad, beaten, wrinkled, and battered by the world.[200]

These tombs, masterpieces of art and sculpture, stand in dramatic contrast with the very simple and humble graves of early Christians generally encountered closer to Peter's grave. The contrast may reflect the difference between the early Christian view of a grave as simply a way station, and the view of the Romans, who believed they would live only in the memory of the living and wished an appropriate final stop. It is certain that all of them, Christians and pagans alike, would be quite surprised to find their final resting places, once on a hill overlooking Eternal Rome, now buried fifteen to sixty feet underground, beneath a massive Christian basilica.

Part of Guarducci's genius was recognizing, preserving, detailing, and opening to experts like Toynbee the Necropolis tombs, so full of history, as well as long-ago hopes and dreams. Yet none of this would save her following Paul VI's death.

CHAPTER NINETEEN

GUARDUCCI ALONE: A NEW BEGINNING

1978

Tennyson's poem "Ulysses" portrays the elderly adventurer, unloved by his people, summoning his aged crew for the final voyage of their lives:

> Death closes all: but something ere the end,
>> Some work of noble note, may yet be done, ...
> Tho' much is taken, much abides; and tho'
>> We are not now that strength which in old days
> Moved earth and heaven, that which we are, we are;
>> One equal temper of heroic hearts,
> Made weak by time and fate, but strong in will
>> To strive, to seek, to find, and not to yield.[201]

Almost exactly nine years after George Strake's death, his great friend Pope Paul VI died outside of Rome. Harkening back to his collaboration with Carroll, McGeough, Kaas, Strake, and Guarducci, Paul VI had only one final request. He wished to duplicate Saint Peter's burial in location and form, being placed directly in the soil without tomb or monument near the location where Peter's bones had been found. Thus he joined Ludwig Kaas, a short distance from the Graffiti Wall.

Without Paul VI's protection, Guarducci would now feel the power of Ferrua and the Vatican bureaucracy. Blunt, without tact, a remarkable scientist but a terrible politician, Guarducci was an easy target. For his part Ferrua, after twenty-six years of humiliation, was intent on a harsh and merciless revenge.

Almost immediately, Ferrua fired Guarducci and excluded her from working on or even visiting the Necropolis or the Graffiti Wall.[202] After a short time, the bones that had been identified as Peter's were quietly removed from public view. Guarducci and the bones disappeared from all new Vatican publications. Vatican guides did not mention them or Guarducci.[203] In effect, Ferrua and the Vatican antiquities bureaucracy overruled *sub silencio* Pope Paul VI's authentication of Guarducci's find. It was a bureaucratic sleight of hand worthy of the Medici, cruel and almost certain to eliminate Guarducci from any further Vatican involvement.[204] When Guarducci or others wrote of her finds, they were greeted either with silence or ridicule, particularly by Ferrua. Yet this apparent end of aged Guarducci's brilliant career was in fact only a new beginning. She would strive, seek, find, and never yield.

Truly, this rejection of her twenty-five years of work would have been enough to destroy any normal person. At the age of seventy-six, she was fired and excluded like a criminal from access to the work she had poured her whole life into for more than two decades.[205] Her work was denounced as the imaginary ramblings of an ignorant, pious woman. These denunciations came not from outsiders, but from leaders within the Church she so deeply loved. It would be twelve years before she could speak publicly of the deep sadness and hurt inflicted upon her by those within the Vatican bureaucracy. But Guarducci was not broken or finished, even at seventy-six. Ferrua apparently did not understand the immense strength of a determined woman. In fact, Guarducci would prove to be an Italian version of the unsinkable Molly Brown, another Annie Taylor.[206] For Guarducci, her end was only a new beginning. Continuing to teach epigraphy and archeology at La Sapienzia University in Rome, Guarducci also repeatedly published or assisted with articles and books defending her finds. Each was met with a savage review attacking her by Ferrua or a surrogate.

Vatican insiders, likely with Ferrua's approval, even secretly leaked Ferrua's own report, *I-XVII and OSSA-U-GRAF*, by giving journalist J. J. Benitez access to the secret archives of the Vatican library.[207] While they would not permit Benitez to copy the *OSSO*, they did allow him to take notes. According to those notes, Ferrua's report contended, "No serious scientist has paid attention to … the information of the pontiff" and "the apostle [could] have been buried anywhere, and even as Roman law for criminals, thrown in the Tiber or buried in a mass grave." The report further maintained that Pius XII had been "deaf" to his advisors when he made his 1949 public announcement that they had found Peter's bones, following the leak by Camille Gianfara. Ferrua's report asserted there was "no scientific evidence" to prove the bones Guarducci had found were Peter's. Paul VI was likewise "deaf" to his advisors. All of this had absolutely no effect on Guarducci's efforts or determination.

Guarducci remained the moving force behind books defending her find, including *The Bones of Saint Peter* by John Evangelist Walsh, published in 1982.[208] However, Ferrua's power inside the Vatican more than trumped her campaign. The bones remained obscured in storage while

Guarducci remained a Vatican nonperson, wholly excluded from the Necropolis. Ferrua periodically led or inspired attacks in which adherents or secularists claimed the bones were a Church-orchestrated fraud, laughable to all experts. The articles relied either on ridicule (for example, focusing on the animal bones found with the Graffiti Wall bones) or on mistaken facts (such as confusing the discredited Ferrua bones with those discovered by Guarducci from the Graffiti Wall).[209]

Meanwhile, a significant new piece of evidence emerged from an unlikely discipline: architecture. The Romans are often called history's greatest engineers. When Constantine's engineers built the original St. Peter's and the original marble box enclosing the Trophy of Gaius, the Graffiti Wall no longer served any architectural or engineering purpose. It could easily have been removed. Yet they chose to leave the Graffiti Wall intact, enclosing it within Constantine's monument. This oddity created an inexplicable and maddening imperfection in an otherwise typically Roman, symmetrical structure. Leaving the Graffiti Wall in place for no apparent engineering reason required that Constantine's architects move their marble box "off center" by eighteen inches (the width of the Graffiti Wall). For hundreds of years, this inexplicable imperfection had been noted with no ready explanation. Really, the only possible explanation is that the fourth-century engineers knew that something very important was contained within the Graffiti Wall.[210]

1990 — Guarducci Builds Her Reputation

The Age of the Great Ideological Tyrannies in Europe melted in Italy into the Age of Fellini, of Gucci, Valentino, Fendi, and Prada. In a stark symbol of the new age of materialism, the fashion house Fendi would acquire Mussolini's masterpiece of Fascist architecture in Rome, turning it into their headquarters. Handbags and shoes would replace the fasces and portraits of Il Duce. As the churches emptied and a deep, skeptical, secular materialism spread throughout Europe, Guarducci herself became living history — an ancient relic from a different age. Excluded from her work in the Vatican, she moved to other places and sites not controlled by Ferrua or his minions, where her genius was apparent. She authenticated ancient objects and discredited others as forgeries. Among other things, she was deeply involved in discrediting as a fake the so-called *Praeneste Fibula — a golden brooch said to bear the earliest Latin inscription.*[211] This remains a heavily debated issue.[212]

The Case of the Black Madonnas

She additionally and simultaneously solved two great mysteries relating to the earliest known image of Jesus' mother, Mary. The first, pre-dating A.D. 438, was known to history as the Madonna Hodegetria.[213] The legendary icon remained in Constantinople for more than a thousand years. Since at least the fifth century, this icon of the Madonna and Child was venerated in Hagia Sophia in Constantinople, the principal church of the Eastern Empire. The vast cathedral, rebuilt twice because of earthquakes, was finally completed in 537 and served for nearly one thousand years as the centerpiece of the Eastern Roman Empire and the Greek Orthodox Church. In 1453, the Turks conquered Constantinople, and the entire city endured three days of looting and pillage, including Hagia Sophia. Along with numerous other artifacts dating back to the dawn of Christianity, the Madonna Hodegetria disappeared (likely pillaged or destroyed). The icon survived only in ancient manuscripts relating its description and special importance to the Greek people. For five hundred years, it was believed forever lost with no surviving copy.

A second seemingly unrelated mystery involved the so-called Black Madonna — now known as the national symbol of Poland. This icon (also known as Our Lady of Czestochowa), housed in the Jasna Gora shrine in Czestochowa, Poland, depicts Mary holding an infant Jesus, both with dark skin. The icon, probably the most venerated object in Poland, had been the inspiration for many Polish victories, including over the Tartars in the 1300s and the Swedes in 1655. It inspired the brave defense of Warsaw in 1920 against the Soviet Communists. Pope Saint John Paul II, the first Polish pope, first pledged his life to the priesthood in the presence of the Black Madonna, which remained a special object of devotion for him throughout his life. As pope, the shrine of the Black Madonna was his principal stop in Poland. Pope Emeritus Benedict XVI[214] and Pope Francis[215] have also made this shrine their key stopping place when visiting the country. But where did the famous icon come from, and when? How was it created and by whom? Wild stories circulated about its origin, but the truth seemed to be lost to history — until Margherita Guarducci got involved.

In a sanctuary called Montevergine, located about four hundred feet above the countryside of Campania, Guarducci (now in her mid-eighties) located an ancient icon called the Madonna of Montevergine. It was also a black icon — a virtually perfect copy of Poland's Black Madonna. Trudging through churches, islands, and ancient hillside monasteries, and conducting extensive research, she proved that the Montevergine icon came to Rome in the seventh century as a gift from the Greek emperor. It was a reverse mirror image copy of the ancient Greek Madonna in the Hagia Sophia at Constantinople. Guarducci was able to prove that the Polish Black Madonna was the very same image as the seventh-century Montevergine icon, and that both were therefore derived from the early Greek Madonna in Constantinople.[216] She thus rediscovered for history both the earliest known image of Mary and the origin of Poland's national symbol.[217] For this and other feats of genius and incredible work, she was hailed as the Grand Dame of Italian Archeology — a living legend and deeply beloved by many of her students. Slowly opinion and science moved her way, despite Ferrua's iron grip on the Necropolis and the Vatican's concern with more pressing matters.

A Tale of Two Statues

For hundreds of years, antiquarians had believed that a statue of Saint Hippolytus at the entrance to the Vatican Library was the oldest Christian statue. Guarducci proved the statue dated only from the Renaissance, circa 1500.[218] Instead, she found substantial evidence that the large, magnificent bronze statue of Peter in the central nave of the Vatican was the oldest known Christian statue — cast and built for a mausoleum of the Roman emperors of the West in the fifth century, before the collapse of the Empire. Even in her late eighties, Guarducci has continued to solve some of the great mysteries of Christian archeology with rare intensity and energy.

Milan

Although her genius and her intense passion for the truth led her into totally unrelated ancient mysteries and places far away, Guarducci always returned to advocate for the truth of her discoveries below the Vatican. Nothing could distract Guarducci's persistent confidence that Paul VI had been correct that she had located Peter's relics. The great battle between Guarducci and Ferrua reached a crescendo in Milan in 1990, twenty years after Paul VI's pronouncement of the authenticity of her great find, and twelve years after her banishment.

The University of Milan invited the eighty-eight-year-old Guarducci to appear in what would be the final live symposium of her life. She was interviewed by Italy's most famous expert on antiquities, Federico Zeri, also a major television figure, a Sotheby expert on antiquities, and another great detective in outing fakes. A nearly blind Guarducci was led onto the stage by her sister. Before a packed audience and television cameras, Guarducci gave an impassioned defense of her life's work. She said she had lived her life following the truth wherever it led, whether or not it corresponded with her faith. She praised the courage of Popes Pius XII and Paul VI in pursuing the truth, while denouncing the insiders at the Vatican who now sought to suppress it.

Zeri then spoke. He quietly said he was not a Christian believer, but for fifty years of his long life he had followed Guarducci's work, before and after her involvement with the Vatican. Zeri described her as a "diamond bit" seeking the truth. He knew her work to be sound and scientific.[219] Unlike her opponents, she did not pursue clientele or ideology, but only the truth. He expressed his opinion based on the scientific evidence that she had indeed found Peter. The audience erupted in cheers.

Margherita Guarducci continued to teach well into her nineties, though she was blind and had to be led into the classroom by her sister. She would recite by heart the ancient Greek inscriptions and texts she had found as long ago as her excavations in the 1920s in Crete. She would also recite by heart many of the Christian inscriptions she found during the Peter excavations. Guarducci would often move her hands in the form of the inscriptions as if remembering when she first encountered them forty to sixty years before. Although blind, she saw them again in her mind's eye as she had long ago found them. In 1995, at the age of ninety-three, she published her final great defense of her discoveries under the Vatican. Although she was now aged and gray, the last pictures of her show the same detached half-smile of amusement, the same strand of pearls around her neck. When her eyesight vanished entirely after her many years in the gray darkness of Crete and the Vatican, she stayed home with her sister at her apartment in Rome. She did not live to see the new millennium. On September 2, 1999, she died and was buried in a cemetery in Rome, a short distance from Dr. Correnti, the anthropologist who had debunked the Ferrua bones and authenticated the Graffiti Wall bones.

The Vatican took no official notice of any kind of her death.

CHAPTER TWENTY

RETURN OF THE APOSTLE

Ferrua's triumph appeared complete and permanent. Anyone else with direct knowledge of the excavations — Popes Pius XII and Paul VI, Carroll, McGeough, Kaas, Strake, and Correnti — had died. Only Ferrua remained, and he held the highest position on matters relating to Vatican antiquities. Despite scientific evidence, Guarducci's persistent and eloquent defense of her finds, and Paul VI's endorsement, the Graffiti Wall bones remained in storage in a papal chapel. The bones went unmentioned by the Vatican guides.

Pope John Paul II was the first non-Italian pope in four centuries. Unlike Pius XII and Paul VI, he was not a Vatican insider. Deeply preoccupied with the struggles of Communism in the East and secularism in the West, he did not share the keen interest of Pius XII and Paul VI in archeology. While John Paul was a deeply inspirational figure for the world and clearly a man for the ages, there is no evidence that the history or working of the Vatican structures themselves held much interest for him. As head of Vatican antiquities, Ferrua held all the cards, and there were not even any other players left at the table. It appeared that the Graffiti Wall bones would once again be wholly forgotten.

In 2003, Ferrua died and was buried at his request and as an honor in the Necropolis below the Vatican, close to where his excavations began sixty-three years earlier. Ferrua and Ludwig Kaas are believed to be the only priests resting in the Necropolis, surrounded by many popes and royal persons, as well as the remains of many hundred ancient Romans. Ferrua was honored by numerous articles, particularly from the secular press, as a hero who prevented the Church from laughably presenting the bones of mice and animals as relics of Saint Peter. Further articles challenged the existence of Peter or expressed doubt that he had ever come to Rome at all. At the time of Ferrua's death, several articles once again viciously ridiculed Guarducci and her find.

Over time, following Ferrua's death, Vatican publications, which had previously ignored Guarducci's great work and failed to mention her at all, began to include mentions of her work, describing it as controversial. It was a definite, although limited promotion from nonperson.[220]

June 2009

With the election of Pope Benedict XVI came a resurgence of serious study of the origin of the gravesites of Peter and Paul, both of whom were executed in Rome by Nero. On June 28, 2009, Pope Benedict confirmed that the gravesite of Paul on the Port Road to Ostia (the place of his beheading) outside the walls of Rome was authentic. Carbon dating of the bones in Paul's tomb proved they were from the first century, confirming them as Paul's authentic remains.[221] Peter's turn would come next.

March 2013

Although both Ferrua and Guarducci were gone, they each continued to have passionately committed advocates. In March 2013, following the retirement of Benedict XVI, Cardinal Jorge Bergoglio was elected pope, taking the name Francis. Within a short time after his election, Francis knelt and prayed in the Necropolis at the location of Peter's purported grave at the Graffiti Wall. He then continued a detailed review of all the evidence gathered by Ferrua, Guarducci, Correnti, and retained experts — much of that evidence fifty years old or even older. The review apparently had been initiated by his predecessor, Benedict. After this review, at a papal Mass in Vatican Square on November 24, 2013, marking the end of the Year of Faith, Pope Francis displayed the Graffiti Wall bones. Clutching them to himself in a case, he announced to the large crowd and the world that these were indeed Peter's relics.[222] A few days later, on December 5, 2013, Pope Francis in a public ceremony returned the bones to public display in the niche in the Graffiti Wall where they had been found more than seventy years before. He once again placed the full weight of the Catholic Church behind their authenticity as Peter's relics. He became the third pope to affirm Peter's burial on Vatican Hill, and thus, in essence, Peter's presence and martyrdom in Rome.

The bones remain today on public display in the Graffiti Wall under the Vatican, accessible through a public entrance off Vatican Square. In the view of the Church, the Apostle's relics have returned home to their proper place near the site where the Apostle gave up his life for his belief in Christ.

CHAPTER TWENTY-ONE

THE GREAT PERSECUTION AND HELENA

Who moved Peter's bones from their resting place under the Trophy of Gaius to the niche in the Graffiti Wall where they resided until 1942? How were they moved? When? As to time, it is clear from the forensic evidence that Peter's bones rested under or near the Trophy from the time of its construction before 150 until sometime between 250 and 337 — as dated by Guarducci. She believed they were most likely moved by Constantine's workers to the marble-lined niche in the Graffiti Wall during the construction of St. Peter's to protect them, given particularly the purple and gold cloth in which they had been wrapped — a cloth used exclusively by the imperial family.

Guarducci may be right, but a much more likely possibility is suggested by the history surrounding the years 250–337. This was a period of horrific persecution of Christians under Emperors Valerian and Diocletian. The persecution by Diocletian is commonly called the Great Persecution because of the cruel and widespread slaughter of Christians. Prior to this period, it was an unthinkable crime for any Roman to disturb a grave — even the grave of a criminal, enemy, or Christian. By edict of Valerian and

Diocletian, however, Christian graves lost their immunity. The emperors made war on the dead, desecrating Christian graves, ironically in the same way their own tombs would later be destroyed by the barbarians. Faced with this danger, it seems quite likely that brave unnamed Christians moved Peter to the Graffiti Wall niche during this period, leaving the hidden inscription, "Peter is here." This is one plausible hypothesis for how the bones were moved.

By this period, Christianity was no longer a small cult. Christians had inexplicably survived ten separate waves of Roman persecution.[223] The Romans still regarded the Christians' faith in an alleged criminal executed by Rome as a direct assault on the *dignitas* of Rome itself. Their persecutions of Christians had been thorough, systematic, and cruel. But the net result of more than two hundred years of Roman assault had been the growth of the small cult into a major underground religion with an estimated five million followers, possibly more — about 5 percent of the population.

By the time Constantine came to power, Christians were a significant minority in the Empire. The Imperial household itself was riddled with Christian believers, even before Constantine. For example, Diocletian, in order to remove Christians, required all members of the army to worship him. His own bodyguard, Sebastian, refused and was apparently executed by a firing squad with arrows and left for dead. After being revived by Christians, instead of fleeing, he sought out Diocletian, publicly condemned him for his cruelty, and was killed. Tradition has it that Pope Caius, who headed the Church during the reign of Diocletian, was a relative of the emperor, but the relationship did not save him. According to unverified legend, he was hunted down, seized in the Roman catacombs, and brutally executed, along with his young niece, Susanna.

Indeed, in the highest ranks of Diocletian's government lived an extraordinarily brave and determined woman who would eventually become a Christian, and her faith would change the course of the Roman Empire forever. Helena, mother of the future emperor Constantine, would be responsible for encouraging her son's faith, eventually leading to the construction of the first St. Peter's Basilica. Born an innkeeper's daughter, an extraordinary beauty, Helena married a young Roman officer named Constantius around 272. He called her his soulmate. She gave birth to his son, Constantine. But as Constantius rose through the ranks, eventually becoming Caesar of the Western Empire, Helena, as a woman of humble birth, became a serious inconvenience. He divorced her around 292, a few years before Diocletian's persecution of Christians began, in order to marry an emperor's daughter. Like Guarducci, Helena was abandoned in a male-dominated world and, except for Constantine, friendless. But like Guarducci, brave Helena had an extraordinary comeback. In 306 her son brought her to his court. Constantine was now Augustus, emperor of the West and soon to be the sole ruler of the whole Roman Empire. Helena was installed as Augusta — the most powerful woman in the world. It is not known when she became a Christian, whether before or after Constantine brought her to court, but she was baptized and became a devout Christian. Later, following the Edict of Milan, she enjoyed unlimited access to the Imperial treasury to pursue her passion for Christian archeology.

She is recognized by the Church as the patron saint of archeologists. Indeed, she was the first Christian archeologist, preserving numerous ancient relics. In 326, at age eighty, she made an epic journey to Jerusalem to preserve ancient Christian relics, establishing churches that are still in existence today. She was deeply involved in the preservation of graves of the apostles, inspiring the construction of St. Peter's in Rome, as well as the construction of a now destroyed basilica over the grave of John the Evangelist outside of Ephesus.

All three of the primary factors employed by a good investigator to prove involvement — motive, opportunity, and a history of similar methods and acts — strongly point to Helena's involvement in the transfer of Peter's bones to the Graffiti Wall. Possibly the move occurred during the horrible persecution of Diocletian, but perhaps it took place during the construction of the basilica, when Guarducci believes they were moved. Helena died in 330, well before the completion of St. Peter's, and Constantine followed not long after. Following their deaths, their families fought over the crown, and the Empire began its slow, century-long death spiral. Very likely, they intended to build the great bronze sarcophagus and 150-pound gold cross that fifth-century accounts said should mark the site of Peter's bones. But mortality and circumstances apparently intervened, and the monument was forgotten.

In a nave on the main floor of the Vatican, there is a shrine to Helena with a wonderful statue of her. Ironically, her statue looks and gestures down, as if pointing for centuries to the unknown Necropolis below. We will likely never know the extent of Helena's involvement in the movement of Peter's bones. There is symmetry, however, in the idea of brave Helena, consumed with a passion for Christian archeology, preserving Saint Peter's relics until their discovery 1,600 years later by another strong and brave woman archeologist.

To many believers, including Blessed Pope Paul VI, it is fitting that the apostle was buried first in the simple earth and then preserved in a simple wall — no gold cross, no great bronze sarcophagus.

AFTERWORD

The great eighteenth-century poet Thomas Gray, musing on a different graveyard in his "Elegy Written in a Country Churchyard," wrote:

> The boast of heraldry, the pomp of power,
>   And all that beauty, all that wealth e'er gave,
> Awaits alike the inevitable hour.
>   The paths of glory lead but to the grave.[224]

Certainly this has proven true in the lives of the Three Amigos.

Aside from the beautiful bell tower dedicated to Walter Carroll by George Strake and others in his hometown of Pittsburgh, and his portrait hanging alongside Strake's in the parish church of St. Philip Neri in Garbatella, there are strangely no memorials, biographies, or other physical remembrances of Walter Carroll, the brave priest who saved thousands of refugees and may well have saved Rome itself from destruction by the Germans and the Allies. In a certain sense, the entire city of Rome today is Carroll's memorial.

Joseph McGeough later served as the Vatican's point man in places as far removed as warring Northern Ireland and segregated South Africa. Yet after his death in 1970, he also strangely seems to have been forgotten.

Montini — Blessed Pope Paul VI — is buried in a simple grave in the earth very near where he believed and proclaimed Peter to have been buried. Among his final words were, "The Tomb: I would like it to be in the real earth, with a humble sign to indicate the place and to invite Christian piety. No monument for me."[225]

The great Conroe Oil Field, after fifty-five million years in existence and almost ninety years of production, is largely spent. The rigs are gone and the wells mostly silent. Production is a fraction of what it was in the 1940s when it fueled the Allies. According to entries on the internet, teens surreptitiously jump a fence to swim in Crater Lake near Conroe, no doubt ignorant that it was once the scene of a massive 1933 explosion. Most are probably ignorant also of the name George Strake. In conformity with his wishes, little was named after George Strake during his life, nor did he seek public acclaim. No Rockefeller Center for George Strake. He would be very glad to know he currently has no entry on Wikipedia. Aside from a monument or two (including the simple one in the parish church in far-off Garbatella), a distinguished high school, and buildings named for him after his death, his great memorials are his family and his deeds.

His children and grandchildren are self-made, each successful in their own way. His namesake grandson once remarked that when he was young, he wished the great fortune (once among the largest in the world) had not been given away. Now older, he realizes the great name and legacy of generosity was a better inheritance. Similarly, a generation later, Strake's great-grandson has asked why the fortune was given away. Hopefully this book answers that question — because George Strake believed in and possessed nobility of character, beyond money, fame, or class. He had a generosity so great that he could not hide it, even with his demands of anonymity, and a faith that did move mountains. From the Pius XII Center at St. Louis University, which now contains copies of materials from the ancient Vatican archives to insure against their loss, to the tens of thousands of campers who have enjoyed his beloved Glen Eyrie and Eagle Lake, his legacy proves that we're meant to use our resources for the good of others. Beyond question, however, his most important and enduring legacy lies in the dark Necropolis below the Vatican.

Margherita Guarducci rests in a cemetery in Rome, only a few yards from the grave of Dr. Venerando Correnti, who authenticated her find.[226] She is regarded as one of the greatest archeologists of the twentieth century. The Christian inscriptions she decoded are perhaps of even greater significance than the discovery of Peter's bones. If once, like Peter, she was lost, now she has been found. In May 2015, the citizens of Rome posthumously honored her by naming a street after her — the "Via Margherita Guarducci" — and testimonials to her recently appeared in various international newspapers.[227] Recently, the Vatican website has also begun to acknowledge her contribution.

Ferrua is buried in the Necropolis only a few yards from where Pope Francis placed the full weight of the Catholic Church behind Guarducci's find. There is no street named for Ferrua, who no doubt rested a bit unquietly during Pope Francis's nearby ceremony in 2013. On Ferrua, one of the few surviving friends of Guarducci remarked: "I don't believe in the old legend of Peter as gatekeeper of Heaven, where I know Margherita is. But if it is so, I wonder how Peter greeted Ferrua."

The Necropolis is no longer the dark, dusty, debris-filled ruin encountered by the excavators and later by Guarducci. The great flood of 1949 has never reoccurred, and the "curse" of the excavation proved illusory. Instead, the Necropolis has been restored and gentrified — even air-conditioned — and opened to visitors. Getting a tour of the Necropolis remains tricky, and visitors must apply many months in advance to the Vatican for tickets. The Necropolis' permanent occupants would no doubt be happy to know that after their sleep of nearly two millennia, the newly opened Vatican tour, known as the Scavi Tour, is widely regarded today as "one of Rome's hottest tickets."[228]

Walking up the ancient hill now deep underground, visitors to the Scavi pass simple Christian graves, finally coming to the strange trophy Gaius wrote of so long ago, flanked by the Red Wall and the Graffiti Wall, with Peter's bones now on display in the niche of the Graffiti Wall. The guides seldom explain the strange scratches on the Graffiti Wall.

As to Peter, an ancient Christian story (later the subject of books and movies) relates that Peter fled Rome to escape Nero's persecution. On his way out of Rome along the Appian Way, he met Christ walking back toward the city. Peter asked the Lord the famous question: "*Quo vadis?*" (Where are you going?) Jesus is said to have answered, "I am going to Rome to be crucified again." Ashamed that Christ was taking his place, Peter turned back to Rome to meet his fate. An ancient church that may date back to the eighth century, called Domine Quo Vadis, marks the site near the Appian Way where this supposedly occurred.

There is no proof of this story, but there is abundant evidence — both early documentary evidence and compelling physical evidence — that Peter was captured and executed by Nero in Rome. This includes the early documentary references to his Roman grave, the early inscriptions around it, the Trophy of Gaius itself and, very compellingly, the epigrams and bones discovered by Guarducci. His body (with his feet cut off after being crucified upside down) was discarded on Vatican Hill where his followers, in great danger, buried him and began to pray at his grave in secret, erecting a trophy over it and writing coded prayers around it.[229] Peter's bones were later moved, either during the great persecutions of Christians by Valerius and Diocletian (after 250 and before the completion of the first St. Peter's in 337) or perhaps, as Guarducci believed, during the construction of Constantine's basilica.[230]

The lengthy excavation project is complete. The great puzzle has been solved. Peter's earthly remains have been returned after seventy-five years to the Graffiti Wall. Where Peter's spirit is and whether all paths of glory really do end at the grave remains, of course, a matter of faith.

Quo vadis?

APPENDICES

Appendix I

The Inscriptions

Margherita Guarducci's decoding of the almost two-thousand-year-old inscriptions on the Graffiti Wall and in other locations in the Necropolis is one of the epic works of epigraphy and archeology. Not only did it lead to the discovery of Peter's relics, but also to a new direct understanding of the actual beliefs of early Christians — proven not through the prism of later writings, but through the physical evidence of their contemporary inscriptions. Before Guarducci, the inscriptions were dismissed by the early excavators as meaningless and indecipherable.

Guarducci's work to understand the inscriptions, which consumed three to five years of her life, is best described in her highly technical 1960 book, *The Tomb of Saint Peter* (Hawthorn), and in her later works like *Peter: The Rock on Which the Church Is Built* (1977, Vatican) and *The Primacy of the Church of Rome* (1991, Rusconi Libri, Milan). Guarducci also wrote many articles from 1958 until 1995 about her discoveries and the remarkable inscriptions she uncovered and deciphered.

The inscriptions on the Graffiti Wall resemble a forest of trees, one overlaid on top of another. Guarducci first used photography and magnification to produce more coherent images. She recognized that the inscriptions represented a code used by early Christians to express religious beliefs in a way indecipherable to their Roman persecutors, and to portray parables and allegories that express profound truths recognizable only to people of faith. Christ himself taught his followers in parables (cf. Matthew 13), such as the Prodigal Son and the Good Shepherd. Early Christian art reflects this, and the Graffiti Wall inscriptions were no different: they spoke by allusion and parable.

Through a careful process of photography, magnification, and actual physical examination in the Necropolis over many months, Guarducci accomplished this tedious task. She was able to identify the actual inscriptions one by one. She surveyed the Roman world and found the same code symbols were often used by early Christians, particularly in Rome, but also in the far reaches of the Empire from the second to the sixth centuries. After long study, she found three keys to breaking this code:

1. Almost every alphabetic phonic symbol had in turn a hidden symbolic meaning.

2. The joining of letters through signs of union expressed religious concepts.

3. The use of symbols over letters combined thoughts. For instance, the letter "P" overlaid with key symbols recalled Peter, keeper of the keys to the Kingdom.

By way of example, Guarducci found on the Graffiti Wall and on an early Christian tombstone elsewhere the letters "TE" together or joined with a line. This symbol reflects the Cross (T) reopening Eden (E) or Paradise. Alpha (A) and Omega (Ω), the first and last Greek letters, reflect the beginning and the end. They appear repeatedly with both symbols of Christ (because Christ is the beginning and the end) and reversed with proper names (this person's end is only his beginning). "RA" meant "I am the Resurrection and the beginning of Life."

These and many other inscriptions appeared not only on the Graffiti Wall, but also on other previously undecipherable inscriptions found in places ranging from the Colosseum to numerous tombstones. At another point on the Graffiti Wall, the Greek word "NICA" (victory) was written directly over the symbols for Christ, Mary (M), and Peter. On the adjoining Red Wall, built around 160, Guarducci found coded inscriptions meaning "Peter is here" — as it turns out, these provided a marker and were not merely a prayer.

The theological implications of the Graffiti Wall to a Christian are profound and moving. Peter occupies a central role in the Church, and it is clear the early Christians honored him and prayed to him for aid. From earliest times, Christians believed in eternal life unlocked by Christ's death on the Cross. Christianity was not simply an evolving cult. By 150–300, the basic tenets of Christianity were believed so deeply that Christians would risk their lives even to inscribe them on a wall marking the site of a martyr's burial.

As Guarducci wrote, "The epigraphs are unusually precious witnesses bringing the direct, live echo of past events." They remain "a voice that we must hear."[231]

Appendix II

The Conroe Oil Field

Scientists believe that more than sixty-five million years ago, an asteroid, believed to measure between 106 and 186 miles in width, struck the ocean offshore of Yucatan, Mexico, leaving an immense crater and killing most of life on Earth, including the dinosaurs. The massive crater was actually located by geologists on the Texas Gulf Coast, who noticed a ring of oil-bearing sands down the Texas Coast which they believed were laid down by an immense tsunami more than 9,800 feet high, produced by the asteroid. The wave was still over 2,000 feet high when it deposited sands in the area of what would someday be the Conroe oil field.[232]

More than twelve million years after the tsunami, the so-called Eocene Age began, and the Conroe field lay at the bottom of the ocean for many million years. Under the ocean, plant and animal life died and settled to the bottom, slowly decaying. There were coral reefs as high as four hundred feet, traced much later in the vicinity of the field. Deep beneath the surface, an unlikely agent would produce a very unlikely formation.

Salt — the same as common table salt — slowly built up, and being lighter than the soil, it began to push its way upward. Think of a fist pushing through layers of napkins. Over long ages, this "fist" of salt produced a dome filled in its center and on its flanks with decaying plant and animal life. Slowly the dome filled at its top with a massive cap of natural gas — highly combustible. Under the gas and sands pushed up by the inexorable movement of salt, the dome filled with oil in immense quantities — millions of years later to be the lifeblood of an emerging industrial civilization. This area, now known as the Conroe field, would rise from the ocean and fall back again many times during the roughly thirty million years after its formation in the Eocene Age.

The search for oil began in the late nineteenth century, beginning first in Pennsylvania with Edwin Drake. It spread to Texas in the twentieth century. The East Texas Oil Field was discovered in 1930. At that time, one certain rule in the oil business (based on numerous dry holes) was that there was no oil east of Conroe. Seismic and other data gathered by the large oil companies proved this. The dry holes and bankrupt dreams of numerous explorers supported the evidence. Meanwhile, the great salt dome, containing incalculably large amounts of gas and oil, waited almost one mile below the earth's surface.

Along came George Strake in 1931. After leasing more than 8,500 acres for a pittance, he went to every major oil company seeking an industry partner. He had none of the detailed seismic data, production history, reservoir engineering, torsion balance, or the like which underlay even the wildest wildcat. His prospect was where repeated dry holes, beginning in 1919, had proven there could be no oil. In addition, seismic and torsion balance data proved this prospect silly and unlikely.

He had only surface evidence: water the cattle would not drink and the anomaly of creeks that flowed the wrong way. The oil companies, with good evidence, believed him a crazy, lone-wolf wildcatter peddling another dry hole. But he believed (as he later said) that he was a team of two with God on his shoulder. He drilled, but hit only the natural gas cap — nearly worthless in those days. There was still no hint of anything below. He drilled again on the flank, and a mile below the surface hit the sea of oil, which had been waiting for him for almost fifty-three million years. The great field's wait was over. Shortly the area above it would become a beehive of human activity.

George Strake died many years before discovery of the great asteroid, confirmed by its vast underwater crater off Yucatan and the layer of iridium dust it deposited seventy-seven million years ago across the Earth. But he would have no problem at all believing that a celestial visitor was the beginning of his great oilfield.

Appendix III

The Story of Vatican Hill

(Diagrams are figurative and not to scale.)

I.

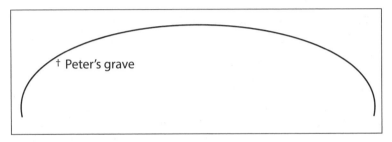

Circa A.D. 64–66: Peter died and was buried on Vatican Hill.

II.

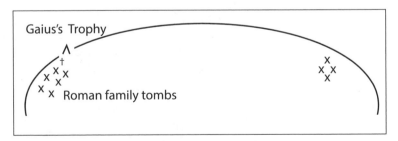

Circa 150: Construction of Gaius's Trophy and many Roman tombs.

III.

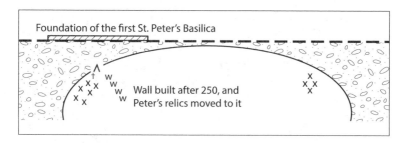

Circa 326: Construction began on the first St. Peter's Basilica. Workers used millions of tons of fill to level the foundation.

IV.

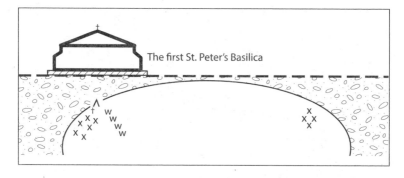

Circa 360: First St. Peter's Basilica completed. The basilica was built centered over the apostle's grave. Except for the encasing of Gaius's Trophy, and following the collapse of Rome in 476, the Necropolis was forgotten. The underground graves slept silently for a thousand years.

V.

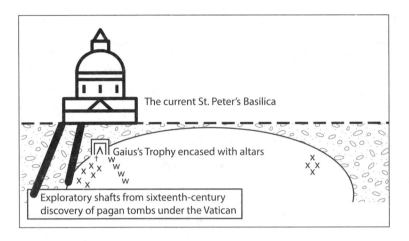

The current St. Peter's Basilica

Gaius's Trophy encased with altars

Exploratory shafts from sixteenth-century
discovery of pagan tombs under the Vatican

1506: Construction began on the new St. Peter's Basilica. The new basilica was built on the old foundation, remaining centered on the apostle's grave. Gaius's Trophy was encased with altars circa 600, 1000, and 1500, but the hill and the forgotten tombs remained unexplored until 1941.

Appendix IV

Timeline

About A.D. 30	Peter meets Jesus and begins to follow him.
64–66	Paul and then Peter are executed in Nero's persecution after the great fire of Rome. Peter's body is discarded on nearby Vatican Hill.
90–300	Many family tombs are built by wealthy Roman families on Vatican Hill.
About 100	Early Christian accounts refer to Peter's burial in Rome.
About 150	A structure is built near Peter's grave by Christians and later written about by Gaius.
250–300	Peter's bones are moved into the Graffiti Wall, either during the late persecutions of Christians or during the construction of Constantine's basilica.
319–333	Construction of the first St. Peter's Basilica by Constantine. Graves and Roman family tombs are covered with fill in order to level the hill.
337–476	Disintegration of the Western Roman Empire. Buried tombs on Vatican Hill are forgotten.
1453	Fall of Constantinople.
1505–1655	Construction of the new St. Peter's Basilica on the old foundation. At least three unsuccessful secret efforts are made to find Peter's tomb.
1939	During the burial of Pius XI beneath the Vatican, Christian and Roman graves are found. Pius XII decides to search for Peter.
1940	Pius's emissary, Father Walter Carroll, secures promise of unlimited financing from George Strake.

1940–1945	Excavations continue secretly despite World War II. Many efforts are made by Carroll to combat Nazis and help the Jews.
1946–1948	Strake works with Carroll on the Italian parish church project. A flood nearly destroys the excavation project under the Vatican.
1950	Pius XII announces the discovery of Peter's tomb and ongoing study of bones found by Ferrua.
1951	Strake visits Rome and meets with the excavators and Pius XII.
1952	Margherita Guarducci is brought into the project and given supervision of it. She begins her study of the inscriptions.
1958	The bones found by Ferrua are determined by forensic exam not to belong to Peter. Pius XII dies.
1962–1965	Extensive testing and other evidence reveal the bones found within the Graffiti Wall to be Peter's. Guarducci decodes the inscriptions.
1966	Pope Paul VI recognizes the bones found within the Graffiti Wall as Peter's.
1978	Paul VI dies and is buried near Peter. Guarducci is fired from the excavation project. The bones Paul VI identified as Peter's are shipped to storage by Father Antonio Ferrua.
1978–1999	Guarducci solves numerous mysteries. Bitter controversy rages between Guarducci and Ferrua over the Graffiti Wall bones.
2013	Following re-examination and additional testing, Pope Francis reaffirms the Church's belief that Guarducci's conclusions indicate that the Graffiti Wall bones were Peter's.

Appendix V

The Hottest Ticket in Rome

Numerous magazine articles call the Scavi Tour "the hottest ticket in Rome," and countless travelers have found it their most interesting tour in Europe. The extraordinary Roman murals and the simple Christian graves transport one back to the height of Roman power and at the same time symbolize the futility and illusion of earthly empires.

The Tour — not suitable for those with claustrophobia — must be arranged well in advance through the Vatican Excavation Office. Requests may be submitted to Scavi@FSP.VA or by fax to +390669873017.

The fortunate traveler who manages to secure a reservation will experience an extraordinarily interesting and deeply inspiring visit.

Notes and Acknowledgments

Notes

1 "The Exclusive Tour of Necropolis below St. Peter's Basilica," *Travel + Style*, March 26, 2015, http://www.travelplusstyle.com/magazine/vatican-top-secret-the-exclusive-tour-of-necropolis-below-st-peters-basilica (accessed April 25, 2017).

2 Caitlin Hurley, "How to score a coveted Scavi Tour of the Vatican Necropolis," *Boston Globe*, February 15, 2014, https://www.bostonglobe.com/lifestyle/travel/2014/02/15/the-tip-how-score-coveted-scavi-tour-vatican-necropolis/9bMrpp2N76Q51ub9mnurAL/story.html (accessed April 25, 2017).

3 "The Exclusive Tour of Necropolis below St. Peter's Basilica."

4 "Vatican Prelate Visiting U.S. Praises Work of America's Catholic Schools and Press," *The Bulletin of the Catholic Laymen's Association of Georgia*, September 22, 1951: 34. Available online at http://scr.stparchive.com/Archive/SCR/SCR09221951p34.php (accessed May 11, 2017).

5 Conversations with the Strake family.

6 "Cardinal Ratti New Pope as Pius XI," New York Times, February 7, 1922, http://query.nytimes.com/mem/archive-free/pdf?res=9D02EED61130EE3ABC4F53DFB4668389639EDE (accessed July 18, 2017).

7 "Know Pio XI Glacier," VisitChile.com, http://www.visitchile.com/en/pio-xi-glacier/ (accessed July 18, 2017).

8 Verlyn Klinkenborg, "The Power of Patagonia," *National Geographic* magazine, February 2010, http://www.nationalgeographic.com/magazine/2010/02/patagonia-southern-chile-torres-del-paine/ (accessed July 18, 2017).

9 John Evangelist Walsh, *The Bones of St. Peter* (Manchester, NH: Sophia Institute Press, 1982), 10. (While Walsh's account is a second-hand source, the information for his book came directly from Margherita Guarducci.)

10 Margherita Guarducci, *The Tomb of St. Peter* (New York: Hawthorn Books, 1960), available online at http://stpetersbasilica.info/Necropolis/MG/TheTombofStPeter-4.htm (accessed May 11, 2017).

11 Margherita Guarducci, *Peter: The Rock on Which the Church Is Built* (Rome, Italy: Rev. Fabbrica di S. Pietro in Vaticano, 1977), 15–16.

12 Lori Pieper, "A Christian Was Here," *On Pilgrimage* (originally published in *Catholic Digest*, May 1992), http://subcreators.com/blog/a-christian-was-here-by-lori-pieper/ (accessed May 11, 2017).

13 "World's earliest surviving Christian inscription identified," CBS News, September 30, 2011, http://www.cbsnews.com/news/worlds-earliest-surviving-christian-inscription-identified/ (accessed August 2, 2017); and Teresa Neumann, "Extremely Rare First-Century Inscription Unearthed in Jerusalem," Breaking Christian News, August 1, 2009, http://www.breakingchristiannews.com/articles/display_art.html?ID=7006 (accessed August 2, 2017).

14 Mary Beard, *SPQR: A History of Ancient Rome* (New York: Liveright, 2015), 518–19.

15 There are many writings relating to the discoveries and excavation. The best of these in English are the following little-known accounts: Margherita Guarducci, *The Tomb of St. Peter* and *Peter: The Rock on Which the Church Is Built*; and the official website of the Vatican on the Tomb of Peter, http://www.vatican.va/roman_curia/institutions_connected/uffscavi/documents/rc_ic_uffscavi_doc_gen-information_20090216_en.html; and popular accounts cited herein on aspects of the story.

16 Thomas J. Craughwell, *St. Peter's Bones* (New York: Random House, LLC/Image, 2013), 95–99; Guarducci, *The Tomb of St. Peter*, 6.

17 Guarducci, *The Tomb of St. Peter*, 33–35 (citing Saint Ignatius of Antioch's letter to the Christians of Rome in A.D. 110, "I do not command you as did Peter and Paul," suggesting that Peter and Paul governed the Church in Rome), and 108; William Steuart McBirnie, Ph.D., *The Search for the Twelve Apostles*, Chapter III, Simon Peter (Carol Stream, IL: 1973); Daniel Iglesias, "San Pedro en el Vaticano. Las pruebas indiscutibles (Margherita Guarducci)," *InfoCatolica*, July 8, 2010, http://infocatolica.com/blog/razones.php/1008071230-san-pedro-en-el-vaticano-las (accessed May 11, 2017).

18 Margherita Guarducci, *The Primacy of the Church of Rome* (San Francisco, CA: Ignatius Press, 1991), 100–111.

19 Eric J. Lyman, "Margherita Guarducci — Are Those Really St. Peter's Bones on Display at the Vatican?" *Sojourners*, December 5, 2013, http://sojo.net/articles/are-those-really-st-peter-s-bones-display-vatican (accessed July 21, 2016).

20 Guarducci, *The Tomb of St. Peter*, 62–63. ("It seemed better, all things considered, to respect the veil of prudent silence which the centuries had woven over St. Peter's tomb and to leave intact in faithful minds a consoling though unproved certitude.")

21 Ibid., 63.

22 Martin Luther, *Against the Roman Papacy Instituted by the Devil* (1545), in Erwin Mülhaupt, *Luther's Evangelien-Auslegung*, II (1947), 551; Guarducci, *The Tomb of St. Peter*, 11; Father Georges de Nantes, "The Truth About the Saint Peter's Tomb," originally published in *CCR*, November 1999, pp. 6–12. Excerpts available at http://crc-internet.org/our-doctrine/catholic-counter-reformation/truth-saint-peter-tomb/ (accessed July 21, 2016).

23 The history of George Strake is recounted in various sources contemporary with his life, and afterward in part in sources such as: Bryan Burrough, *The Big Rich: The Rise and Fall of the Greatest Texas Oil Fortunes* (New York: Penguin Books, Ltd., 2010). Given his lifelong insistence on secrecy, the cooperation of his family — particularly his wonderful son, George Strake Jr. (a legend in his own right) — was extraordinarily helpful in documenting Strake's amazing life and participation with Pius XII, Paul VI, Monsignor Walter Carroll, Father Ludwig Kaas, and Father Joseph McGeough.

24 Henry Ford and Samuel Crowther, *My Life and Work* (Garden City, NY: Garden City Publishing Company, Inc., 1922), 72.

25 "Petros," Greek Names, https://www.greek-names.info/petros/ (accessed August 1, 2017).

26 Reza Aslan, *No god but God: The Origins, Evolution, and Future of Islam* (NY: Random House, 2005).

27 F. F. Bruce, New *Testament* History (New York: Doubleday, 1969), 410.

28 Martin Luther, *Against the Roman Papacy Instituted by the Devil* (Wittenberg, 1545), in E. Mulhaupt, *Luther's Evangelien-Anslagung*, II (1947), 551; Guarducci, *The Tomb of St. Peter*, 11; Fr. Georges de Nantes, *The Truth about the Saint Peter's Tomb*, crc-internet.org, *The Catholic Counter-Reformation in the 21st Century* (November 1999), 6–12, July 21, 2016, crc-internet.org/our-doctrine/catholic-counter-reformation/truth-saint-peter-tomb/ (accessed August 1, 2017).

29 "The Conspiracies of the Roman Emperor Nero," (transcript), Prezi, July 11, 2011, https://prezi.com/p3luqn-z9xfc/the-conspiracies-of-the-roman-emperor-nero/ (accessed August 1, 2017).

30 Angelo Albani and Massimo Astrua, "¿Está enterrado realmente san Pedro en el Vaticano?" Aleteia, November 22, 2013, https://es.aleteia.org/2013/11/22/esta-enterrado-realmente-san-pedro-en-el-vaticano/ (accessed May 11, 2017) ("Is Peter Really Buried in the Vatican?"). Originally published in Italian at FlosCarmeli.net.

31 "Most estimates for Rome's population seem to cluster around 1 million at its height (1st Century BC–2nd Century AD).... No other Western city reached this size for 2000 years." Gregory S. Aldrete, *Daily Life in the Roman City: Rome, Pompeii and Ostia* (Greenwood Publishing Group, 2004,) 22.

32 "The Burning of Rome, 64 AD," eyewitnesstohistory.com (1999), http://www.eyewitnesstohistory.com/rome.htm (accessed October 3, 2016). Tacitus, describing the great fire wrote, "Terrified, shrieking women, helpless old and young, people intent on their own safety, people unselfishly supporting invalids or waiting for them, fugitives and lingerers alike — all heightened the confusion. When people looked back, menacing flames sprang up before them or outflanked them. When they escaped to a neighboring quarter, the fire followed — even districts believed remote proved to be involved."

33 Guarducci, *The Tomb of St. Peter*, 31.

34 John Curran, "The Bones of Saint Peter?" *Classics Ireland*, Vol. 3 (Classical Association of Ireland, 1996), 2.

35 Guarducci, *The Tomb of St. Peter*, 47; Pietro Zander, *The Necropolis under St. Peter's Basilica in the Vatican* (Rome, Italy: Fabbrica di San Pietro, 2009), 10.

36 Guarducci, *Peter: The Rock on Which the Church Is Built*, 8.

37 Ibid. and *The Tomb of St. Peter*, 31; Walsh, *The Bones of St. Peter*, 36.

38 Zander, *The Necropolis under St. Peter's Basilica in the Vatican*, 10.

39 Aubrey Menen, "St. Peter's," *National Geographic* (December 1971), 872. Print. See also "The Bones of St. Peter," *The Angelus Online,* February 2015, http://www.angelusonline.org/index.php?section=articles& subsection=show_article&article_id=3656 (accessed May 11, 2017), referring to Gaius's dialogue repeated in Eusebuis, *Historia Ecclesiastica*, II.25.7, available at http://www.newadvent.org/fathers/250102.htm (accessed May 11, 2017); Guarducci, *Peter: The Rock on Which the Church Is Built*, 8.

40 Michele Basso, *Guide to the Vatican Necropolis* (Rome, Italy: Fabbrica di San Pietro, 1986), 8.

41 Guarducci, *The Tomb of St. Peter*, 38; Pieper, "A Christian Was Here"; Basso, *Guide to the Vatican Necropolis*, 8.

42 Pieper, "A Christian Was Here."

43   Guarducci, *The Tomb of St. Peter*, 124; The Seminarian Guides, North American College, "St. Peter's Basilica," www.stpetersbasilica.info/Docs/seminarians2.htm (accessed October 3, 2016).

44   David F. Wright, "313 The Edict of Milan," *Christianity Today*, Issue 28: 100, http://www.christianitytoday.com/history/issues/issue-28/313-edict-of-milan.html (accessed May 12, 2017).

45   Guarducci, *The Tomb of St. Peter*, 79.

46   Ibid., 64; and *Peter: The Rock on Which the Church Is Built*, 11.

47   Guarducci, *The Tomb of St. Peter*, 54.

48   Thomas Babington Macaulay, "Horatius at the Bridge," in Bliss Carman et al., eds., *The World's Best Poetry* Vol. VII, *Descriptive: Narrative*, 1904, www.bartleby.com/360/7/158.html (accessed July 21, 2016).

49   Richard Cavendish, "The Visigoths Sack Rome," *History Today*, August 8, 2010, http://www.historytoday.com/richard-cavendish/visigoths-sack-rome (accessed October 3, 2016); and Umberto Leoni and Giovanni Staderini, *On the Appian Way: A Walk from Rome to Albano* (Rome: R. Bemporad, 1907), 20–22.

50   Margherita Guarducci, "The Necropolis under the Basilica," in *The Tomb of St. Peter* (Hawthorn Books, 1960), www.stpetersbasilica.info/Necropolis/MG/TheTombofStPeter-4.htm.

51   Guarducci, *The Tomb of St. Peter*, 60.

52   Guarducci, *Peter: The Rock on Which the Church Is Built*, 23; and *The Tomb of St. Peter*, 62.

53   Indianapolis Museum of Art, "Funerary Monument of Flavius Agricola," http://collection.imamuseum.org/artwork/31732/ (accessed May 12, 2017).

54   McBirnie, *The Search for the Twelve Apostles*, 35. (Challenging Luther's speculation, McBirnie writes, "Christian tradition has been in agreement from the earliest times that Peter died in Rome.")

55   King James II was the last Stuart King of England — also the last Catholic king.

56   Christina's story is itself extraordinary. She arguably ranks with Elizabeth I of England, Maria Theresa of Austria, and Catherine of Russia among the most powerful women of her age.

57   Guarducci, *The Tomb of St. Peter*, 63.

58 Guarducci, *Peter: The Rock on Which the Church Is Built, 15; and The Tomb of St. Peter*, 72; Walsh, *The Bones of St. Peter*, 11–12.

59 "Dormit in pace" is an early form of the later Latin *requiescat in pace* ("may he/she rest in peace"), in wide Christian use from earliest times. See "Necropolis (Scavi) Tomb F: The First Tomb of the Caetennii," http://stpetersbasilica.info/Necropolis/TombF.htm (accessed May 12, 2017).

60 School Essay of Eugenio Pacelli to Professor Ignazio Bassi, 1889, cited in "Early Life of Pope Pius XII," Wikipedia (citing Ilse Lore Konopatzki, *Eugenio Pacelli: Pius XII. Kindheit und Jugend*, 1974), en.wikipedia.org/wiki/Early_life_of_Pope_Pius_XII#cite_note-8 (accessed July 21, 2016).

61 Fr. George W. Rutler, "The Tragic Heroism of Pope Pius XII," in *Crisis* magazine, October 22, 2012, www.crisismagazine.com/2012/the-tragic-heroism-of-pope-pius-xii (accessed July 21, 2016).

62 Robert Murphy, *Diplomat Among Warriors* (Garden City, NY: Double Day, 1964), 205.

63 James Akin, "How Pius XII Protected Jews," *Catholic Answers*, May 16, 2016. https://www.catholic.com/magazine/print-edition/how-pius-xii-protected-jews (accessed May 9, 2017).

64 Rabbi Lapide, quoted in Jimmy Akin, "How Pius XII Protected Jews," *Catholic Answers*, May 16, 2016, https://www.catholic.com/magazine/print-edition/how-pius-xii-protected-jews (accessed July 18, 2017).

65 Pope Pius XII, quoted in Joseph Bottum, "The End of the Pius Wars," *First Things* magazine, April 2004, https://www.firstthings.com/article/2004/04/001-the-end-of-the-pius-wars (accessed May 9, 2017).

66 Curran, "The Bones of Saint Peter?" 5.

67 Thomas J. Craughwell, *St. Peter's Bones* (New York: Image, 2013), 2.

68 Lizzy Davies, "Saint Peter's Bones: Vatican Exhumes Old Argument with Plan to Show 'Relics,'" *The Guardian*, November 18, 2013; Tom Mueller, "Inside Job," *The Atlantic*, October 2003, https://www.theatlantic.com/magazine/archive/2003/10/inside-job/302801/ (accessed July 21, 2016).

69 Walsh, *The Bones of St. Peter*, 78; Mueller, "Inside Job."

70 "March 18th 1970 — Kirschbaum Engelbert," http://www.con-spiration.de/syre/english/mar/e0328.html (accessed July 18, 2017); and Obituary of Engelbert Kirschbaum, March 28, 1970, www.con-spiration.de/syre/english/mar/e0328.html (accessed July 21, 2016).

71   Michael Labahn and Bert Jan Lietaert Peerbolte, *Wonders Never Cease: The Purpose of Narrating Miracle Stories in the New Testament and Its Religious Environment* (London: T&T Clark International, 2006), 27.

72   Guarducci, *The Tomb of St. Peter*, 41; Craughwell, *St. Peter's Bones*, 38; "The Bones of St. Peter," Angelusonline.org; and "Dedication of the Churches of St. Peter and St. Paul at Rome," Feast: November 18, EWTN, https://www.ewtn.com/library/MARY/PETEPAUL.HTM (accessed August 2, 2017).

73   Guarducci, *The Tomb of St. Peter*, 88.

74   Louise Ropes Loomis, trans., *The Book of the Popes* (Liber Pontificalis) (New York: Columbia University Press, 1916).

75   Ibid., 72.

76   Guarducci, *The Tomb of St. Peter*, 64.

77   "Was St. Peter in Rome?" Catholic Apologetics Information, www.catholicapologetics.info/apologetics/general/rome.htm (accessed October 3, 2016).

78   Ibid.

79   Walsh, *The Bones of St. Peter*, 17–19; Dan Burstein and Arne de Keijzer, *Inside Angels & Demons: The Unauthorized Guide to the International Best Seller* (New York: Vanguard Press, 2004), 52.

80   Guarducci, *The Tomb of St. Peter*, 69–70.

81   Ibid., 70–73; Walsh, *The Bones of St. Peter*, 19–23.

82   Guarducci, *The Tomb of St. Peter*, 146.

83   Ibid., 142–43, 147.

84   Curran, "The Bones of Saint Peter?" 6.

85   Ibid., 10; Davies, "Saint Peter's Bones."

86   Guarducci, *The Tomb of St. Peter*, 74.

87   Walsh, *The Bones of St. Peter*, 24 (depicting the Rape of Persephone).

88   Guarducci, *The Tomb of St. Peter*, 74.

89   Walsh, *The Bones of St. Peter*, 25–26.

90   Guarducci, *Peter*, 13; and *The Tomb of St. Peter*, 91.

91   Guarducci, *The Tomb of St. Peter*, 90–91.

92 "The Bones of St. Peter" (referring to Gaius's letter repeated in Eusebuis's *Historia Ecclesiastica*, II 25, 7), Angelusonline.org.

93 Guarducci, *The Tomb of St. Peter*, 183; and *Peter*, 26; Iglesias, "San Pedro en el Vaticano. Las pruebas indiscutibles (Margherita Guarducci)."

94 Guarducci, "La verità della tomba di san Pietro," Liturgia della Domenica, originally published in *Tracce. Litterae Communionis*, XXVI, October 1999, pp. 72–77, http://liturgiadomenicale.blogspot.com/2008/06/margherita-guarducci-la-verit-della.html (accessed May 12, 2017).

95 Guarducci, *The Tomb of St. Peter*, 183. The excavators would find four altars built under the high altar of St. Peter's and above a dirt grave dug during the first century: In descending order: (1) the altar of Clement VIII (1592–1605); (2) the altar of Callistus II (1119–1124); (3) the altar of St. Gregory the Great (590–604); and (4) the shrine identified with the Troparion of Gaius (about A.D. 160).

96 Ibid., 81.

97 Ibid., 132.

98 Mueller, "Inside Job."

99 Thomas J. Craughwell, "Relics of the Church's first pontiff finally on display," OSV *Newsweekly*, November 21, 2013, https://www.osv.com/OSVNewsweekly/Faith/Article/TabId/720/ArtMID/13628/ArticleID/13458/Relics-of-the-Church%E2%80%99s-first-pontiff-finally-on-display.aspx (accessed May 12, 2017).

100 Zander, *The Necropolis under St. Peter's Basilica in the Vatican*, 114–15.

101 Guarducci, *The Tomb of St. Peter*, 88.

102 Ibid.

103 Interestingly, Gaius and others called it a "tropaia" — trophy. See Guarducci, *The Tomb of St. Peter*, 41. It was to mark Peter's victory: gaining eternal life through faith — not sadness over one crucified as a common criminal.

104 Guarducci, *The Tomb of St. Peter*, 88.

105 Curran, "The Bones of St. Peter?" 12.

106 Guarducci, *Peter*, 24.

107 "Secret Life of Msgr. Carroll," *The Voice*, November 25, 1983, p. 8.

108 Craughwell, *St. Peter's Bones*, 61. ("According to Israeli diplomat, historian, and theologian Pinchas Lapide, Pope Pius had thousands of Jews concealed in monasteries, convents, and churches across Rome, with as many as three thousand sheltering in Castel Gandolfo, the pope's summer residence.") See also William Doino Jr., "Yad Vashem Honors Cardinal Who Fought for Jewish Lives," *First Things*, December 29, 2012, https://www.firstthings.com/blogs/firstthoughts/2012/12/yad-vashem-honors-cardinal-for-sheltering-jews (accessed July 21, 2016). This article references Popes Pius XI and Pius XII as being special defenders of the Jewish population during WWII.

109 Sacred Heart Church, Pittsburgh, *The Monsignor Walter S. Carroll Memorial Bell Tower* (1934), 19–20; John Franko, "Future pope visited Pittsburgh," Catholic Diocese of Pittsburgh, October 17, 2014, http://www.dioceseofpgh.org/pittsburgh-catholic/future-pope-visited-pittsburgh (accessed May 12, 2017).

110 "By 1942, with the increased wartime demand for crude, production rose, and by 1944 crude yields soared to an all-time annual high of 23,207,917 barrels of oil as gas production surged to 2,930,385,000 cubic feet." "Conroe Oilfield," Texas State Historical Association, https://tshaonline.org/handbook/online/articles/doc02 (accessed July 18, 2017).

111 "Secret Life of Msgr. Carroll," 8.

112 A few surviving statements from a Pittsburgh area bank show Father Carroll's use of at least one account there for Rome projects during the last two years of WWII through the end of 1949. While clearly from a U.S. source with substantial resources, no records could be found identifying the source of the funding of these accounts.

113 Sylvia Hart, "Priest aided Allies as spy in World War II, according to recently revealed papers," *Mobile Christian-Jewish Dialogue*, March 10, 1984, mobilecjdialogue.org/archive1/B_0139.pdf (accessed July 27, 2016).

114 "Giovanni Montini was no stranger to American intelligence. During World War II, he worked in the Office of the Papal Secretariat and passed information to a grateful OSS." In Martin A. Lee, "Their Will Be Done," *Mother Jones*, July/August 1983, www.motherjones.com/politics/1983/07/their-will-be-done (accessed July 21, 2016).

115 Mrs. Anna B. Crow, "Professor Kemon, guest speaker at Jewish-Christian dialogue," February 24, 1984, http://mobilecjdialogue.org/archive1/B_0140.pdf (accessed July 18, 2017).

116 "Bombshell Diaries Opened, Vatican priest's diaries in Miami show Jews aided," *The Voice*, October 8, 1982, p. 6.

117 Franko, "Future pope visited Pittsburgh."

118 "Secret Life of Msgr. Carroll," 8; "Casa O'Toole: A History of the Villa that has become an integral part of the Pontifical North American College," Pontifical North American College Magazine (Summer 2008), p. 12. Print. Available online at https://issuu.com/pnac/docs/summer2008 (accessed May 12, 2017).

119 "Bombshell Diaries Opened," 6.

120 Ibid., 1, 6.

121 "Casa O'Toole," 12. This remains a project of the Strake Foundation.

122 Burke Walsh, "Jews Call Pius XII 'Our Pope,'" *The Guardian*, July 1944, p. 7, available online at arc.stparchive.com/Archive/ARC/ARC07071944p01.php (accessed May 12, 2017); "Bombshell Diaries Opened," 6.

123 Joe Carroll, "The Kerry Monsignor Who Defied the Nazis," *The Irish Times*, April 5, 2008, www.irishtimes.com/news/the-kerry-monsignor-who-defied-the-nazis-1.910330 (accessed August 24, 2016).

124 "Secret Life of Msgr. Carroll," 8; Doino, "Yad Vashem Honors Cardinal," 1–3; Franko, "Future pope visited Pittsburgh."

125 "Secret Life of Msgr. Carroll," 8; *The Monsignor Walter S. Carroll Memorial Bell Tower*, 23.

126 *The Monsignor Walter S. Carroll Memorial Bell Tower*, 32–33.

127 Hart, "Priest aided Allies as spy in World War II."

128 Ibid. (citing George Kemon from Walter Carroll's diary).

129 James Walsh, "Future Pope, 3 Americans Halted Red Tide in Rome," *The Voice,* June 28, 1963, p. 9.

130 "ITALY: Fateful Day," *TIME* magazine, March 22, 1948, http://content.time.com/time/magazine/article/0,9171,804484,00.html (accessed December 13, 2017).

131 Walsh, "Future Pope, 3 Americans Halted Red Tide in Rome."

132 "St. Peter's Alleged Bones Carry 'Curse' but Draw Crowds," *Doubtful News*, November 15, 2013, doubtfulnews.com/2013/11/st-peters-bones-carry-curse-and-draw-the-crowds/ (accessed July 21, 2016); "Dossier: The Tomb of St Peter, digilander.libero.it/nousland/The%20real%20Peter's%20Tomb.html (accessed July 21, 2016).

133   Doyle Murphy, "St. Peter's bones displayed," *New York Daily News*, November 24, 2013, http://www.nydailynews.com/news/world/vatican-bones-st-peter-article-1.1527537 (accessed July 18, 2017).

134   Epigraph of William Shakespeare's Tombstone, "William Shakespeare," Poets' Graves, http://www.poetsgraves.co.uk/shakespeare.htm (accessed May 12, 2017).

135   Walsh, *The Bones of St. Peter*, 52–53 (see image 3), 83, and 118.

136   Ibid.; J. J. Benitez, "Dos Pedros y una Petra," JJBenitez.com, http://www.planetabenitez.com/IOI/historias22.htm (accessed May 3, 2017).

137   Angelus A. DeMarco, *The Tomb of St. Peter: A Representative and Annotated Bibilography of the Excavations* (Leiden, Netherlands: E. J. Brill, 1964), 163.

138   "Bombshell Diaries Opened," 1 & 6 (quoting Carroll's biographer, George Kemon).

139   *The Monsignor Walter S. Carroll Memorial Bell Tower*, 24–33; Franko, "Future pope visited Pittsburgh."

140   "Pope Paul VI Visited U.S. Twice, Has Deep Interest in Church Here," *The Voice* (5), June 28, 1963, pp. 1–2.

141   Franko, "Future pope visited Pittsburgh."

142   Andria De Stefano and Ann Rodgers, "Pittsburgh priest had role in liberation of Rome in 1944," *Pittsburgh Catholic*, June 7, 2016, www.pittsburghcatholic.org/News/Pittsburgh-priest-had-role-in-liberation-of-Rome-in-1944--15161412 (accessed August 24, 2016); Franko, "Future pope visited Pittsburgh"; and Jeff Ostrowski, "The Popes and Bishop Rene H. Gracida," *Views from the Choir Loft*, September 23, 2013, http://www.ccwatershed.org/blog/2013/sep/23/bishop-rene-h-gracida-popes/ (accessed July 18, 2017).

143   Margherita Guarducci, *The Primacy of the Church of Rome*. Guarducci was a professor at La Sapienza di Roma University and member of various academies, including the British Academy and the Accademia dei Lincei.

144   Donald Haggis and Carla Anonaccio, *Classical Archeology in Context: Theory and Practice in Excavation in the Greek World* (Berlin/Boston: Walter de Gruyter GmbH & Co. KG, 2015), 31.

145   Lorenzo Bianchi, "A Life in the Footsteps of Peter," 30Days, September 1999.

146 Paul Risso, *Quanti Sono: I Siti Catholic on Italia*, November 12, 2009.

147 Kenneth W. Harl, *Great Ancient Civilizations of Asia Minor* (Chantilly, Virginia: The Great Courses, 2013), Lecture No. 6. Audiobook. See also Sam Dickson, "German businessman, blew up 9 levels of archaeological remains with dynamite, including the level that is believed to be the historical Troy," *Vintage News*, May 10, 2016, https://www.thevintagenews .com/2016/05/10/german-businessman-blew-up-9-levels-of-archaeological-remains-with-dynamite-including-the-level-that-is-believed-to-be-the-historical-troy/ (accessed July 18, 2017);

148 Salvatore Vicario, "Margherita Guarducci," *Wall Street International*, June 25, 2015, wsimag.com/it/cultura/16101-marherita-guarducci (accessed July 21, 2016).

149 Iglesias, "San Pedro en el Vaticano. Las pruebas indiscutibles (Margherita Guarducci)," 8.

150 Walsh, *The Bones of St. Peter*, 86; Burstein, 53; John Thavis, *The Vatican Diaries: A Behind-the-Scenes Look at the Power, Personalities and Politics at the Heart of the Catholic Church* (New York: Penguin Group (USA), Inc. 2013), 136.

151 Walsh, *The Bones of St. Peter*, 86.

152 Obituary of Father Engelbert Kirschbaum, March 28, 1970, http://www.con-spiration.de/syre/english/mar/e0328.html (accessed October 6, 2016).

153 Nantes, "The Truth about the Saint Peter's Tomb"; Thavis, *The Vatican Diaries*.

154 Pina Baglioni, "'Peter is Here' An Adventure in the Vatican Grottoes," *Traces*, n. 11, January 12, 2013, archivio.traces-cl.com/2013/12/peterihere.html (accessed July 21, 2016).

155 Guarducci, *Peter*, 34; Angelo Albani and Massimo Astrua, "¿Está enterrado realmente san Pedro en el Vaticano?"; and Eyder Peralta, "Vatican Puts St. Peter's Bones on Display for the First Time," NPR, November 24, 2013, http://www.npr.org/sections/thetwo-way/2013/11/24/247027889/vatican-puts-bones-of-st-peter-on-display-for-the-first-time (accessed July 18, 2017).

156 Mueller, "Inside Job."

157 "The battle over the bones, which pits a rigorous Jesuit archaeologist against a pioneering female epigraphist, is one of the

strangest stories to have come out of the Vatican during the 20th century and may also be one of the least dignified." In Davies, "Saint Peter's bones: Vatican exhumes old argument with plan to show 'relics,'" *The Guardian,* November 18, 2013; Curran, "The Bones of Saint Peter?" 1; Salvatore Izzo, "L'Ossservatore Romano recalls the dispute over the bones of St. Peter," Papa Ratzinger blog, July 20, 2012, http://paparatzinger5blograffaella.blogspot. it/2012/07/losservatore-romano-ricorda-la-disputa.html (accessed May 12, 2017); John Curran, "The Rev Antonio Ferrua," *Independent,* August 3, 2003, www.independent.co.uk/news/obituaries/the-rev-antonio-ferrua-36872.html (accessed May 12, 2017); Mueller, "Inside Job."

158 Curran, "The Bones of Saint Peter?"; McBirnie, *The Search for the Twelve Apostles.*

159 Thavis, *The Vatican Diaries*; Menen, "St. Peter's," 874.

160 Guarducci, Peter, 33; and *The Tomb of St. Peter,* 123.

161 Guarducci, *The Tomb of St. Peter,* 100.

162 Ibid., 102–47.

163 Ibid., 90–103.

164 Luis Español Bouché "Margherita Guarducci: buscando a San Pedro," *ReligiónenLibertad,* December 22, 2012, http://www.religionenlibertad .com/margherita-guarducci-buscando-a-san-pedro-26653.htm (accessed May 12, 2017); Guarducci, *The Tomb of St. Peter.*

165 Guarducci, *The Tomb of St. Peter,* 94–95.

166 Ibid., 94.

167 Paolo Risso, "Margherita Guarducci," *Santi Beati,* December 11, 2009, http://www.santiebeati.it/dettaglio/95086 (accessed May 12, 2017).

168 Nantes, "The Truth about the Saint Peter's Tomb."

169 Guarducci, *The Tomb of St. Peter,* 135.

170 Curran, "The Bones of St. Peter?" 10.

171 Walsh, *The Bones of St. Peter,* 101.

172 Curran, "The Bones of St. Peter?" 9; Fr. Roger J. Landry, "Hidden Treasure," *CatholiCity,* May 2, 2008, www.catholicity.com/commentary/ landry/00644.html (July 21, 2016).

173 Menen, "St. Peter's," 872.

174 Craughwell, *St. Peter's Bones,* 84.

175 Craughwell, *St. Peter's Bones,* 85.

176 Walsh, *The Bones of St. Peter*, 107; Baglioni, "'Peter is Here': An Adventure in the Vatican Grottoes"; Guarducci, *The Tomb of St. Peter*.

177 Menen, "St. Peter's," 874.

178 Baglioni, "'Peter is Here' An Adventure in the Vatican Grottoes," 2.

179 Nantes, "The Truth about the Saint Peter's Tomb."

180 Iglesias, "San Pedro en el Vaticano. Las pruebas indiscutibles (Margherita Guarducci)."

181 Bouché, "Margherita Guarducci: buscando a San Pedro."

182 "We can now say that in the investigation of St. Peter's tomb Science has come to the aid of Faith. This happy alliance has placed on age-old tradition a strengthened and renewed seal of irrefutable Truth." In Guarducci, *The Tomb of St. Peter*, 183; Nantes, "The Truth about the Saint Peter's Tomb." See also Walsh, *The Bones of St. Peter*, 119.

183 Benitez, "Dos Pedros y una Petra."

184 Eric J. Lyman, "St. Peter's Bones Fake? Questions Raised about Authenticity of Vatican Relics," *Huffington Post*, December 5, 2013, pp. 1–2, available online at http://www.huffingtonpost.com/2013/12/05/st-peters-bones-fake_n_4393739.html (accessed May 12, 2017); Davies, "Saint Peter's bones: Vatican exhumes old argument with plan to show 'relics'" (citing John Thavis, *The Vatican Diaries*, referring to the excavations as "an embarrassment" for the Church); "Petrus Romanus Pope Francis Perpetuates the Petrine Ploy," *Logos Apologia*, April 2, 2013, www.logosapologia.org/petrus-romanus-pope-francis-perpetuates-the-petrine-ploy/ (accessed July 21, 2016); "Dem Bones, Dem Bones, Dem Dry Bones," *Frankincense and Mirth*, November 30, 2013, www.frankincenseandmirth.com/tag/turkey (accessed July 21, 2016); "Pius XII Announced Discovery of Peter's Tomb," Christianity.com, www.christianity.com/church/church-history/timeline/1901-2000/pius-xii-announced-discovery-of-peters-tomb-11630802.html (accessed July 21, 2016).

185 Benitez, "Dos Pedros y una Petra."

186 Craughwell, *St. Peter's Tomb*, 99–100; Mueller, "Inside Job," 6.

187 Mueller, "Inside Job."

188 Guarducci, *The Tomb of St. Peter*, 172; Edgar R. Smothers, S.J., "The Excavations under Saint Peter's," Theological Studies, Inc. for the Theological Faculties of the Society of Jesus in the United States, Vol. 17 No. 3. September 1956, cdn.theologicalstudies.net/27/27.1/27.1.4.pdf (accessed July 27, 2016); Lyman, "St. Peter's Bones Fake?"

189   Guarducci, *Peter*, 41.

190   Benitez, "Dos Pedros y una Petra."

191   Eyder Peralta, "Vatican Puts St. Peter's Bones on Display for the First Time"; Lyman, "St. Peter's Bones Fake?", citing Lorenzo Bianchi, a leading archaeologist and expert on Church relics, "There are many ways to verify and I suppose there is no way to be 100 percent sure, but from circumstances and records, we can say some specific things about these bones: that they were buried there some time between 114 and 120 AD, that Constantine believed them to be authentic, that other records seem to support that. I think we can be as certain as we can reasonably expect to be about this."

192   "The Rev Antonio Ferrua," Telegraph, May 29, 2003, www .telegraph.co.uk/news/obituaries/1431338/The-Rev-Antonio-Ferrua.html (accessed July 21, 2016).

193   Craughwell, *St. Peter's Bones*, 81.

194   In 1957, Strake was included on *Forbes'* list of fifty richest Americans. In 1966, he was picked by *Life* magazine as the largest U.S. philanthropist. These were both honors he would have happily declined, if possible.

195   Menen, "St. Peter's."

196   Epigraph on Secundula's Tomb.

197   Regina Lee Gee, "The Vatican Necropolis: Ritual, Status and Social Identity in the Roman Chamber Tomb" (Ph.D. dissertation, the University of Texas at Austin, August 2003), p. 175.

198   Ibid., 178–83.

199   Ibid., 132.

200   Ibid., 144–45.

201   Alfred Lord Tennyson, "Ulysses," available at Poetry Foundation, poetryfoundation.org/poems-and-poets/poems/detail/45392 (accessed July 21, 2016).

202   Tom Mueller, "Inside Job," *The Atlantic*, October 2003, https:// www.theatlantic.com/magazine/archive/2003/10/inside-job/302801/ (accessed August 2, 2017).

203   The author toured the Necropolis in 2005. There was no mention of either Guarducci or the inscriptions by the guide.

204   Thavis, *The Vatican Diaries*.

205   Mueller, "Inside Job."

206   Molly Brown, builder of the Brown Palace in Denver, was famous for forcing her lifeboat back at gunpoint to rescue passengers of the *Titanic* from the freezing ocean. Annie Taylor, who could not swim, is famous for her 1901 trip over Niagara Falls in a barrel.

207   Benitez, "Dos Pedros y una Petra."

208   Walsh, *The Bones of St. Peter.*

209   Tom Mueller, "Inside Job," *The Atlantic*, October 2003, www .theatlantic.com/magazine/archive/2003/10/inside-job/302801   (accessed July 18, 2017).

210   Landry, "Hidden Treasure."

211   Archaelogical Institute of America, "Who Made the Praeneste Fibula?" *Archaeology*, 2009, archive.archaeology.org/online/features/ hoaxes/praeneste_fibula.html (accessed July 21, 2016); Arthur E. Gordon, "Review: *La cosiddetta Fibula Prenestina. Antiquari, eruditi e falsari nella Roma dell' Ottocento* by Margherita Guarducci," *The Classical Journal*, vol. 78, no. 1 (October–November, 1982), pp. 64–70, available online at www .jstor.org/stable/3297269?seq=1 (accessed July 21, 2016).

212   Vicario, "Margherita Guarducci."

213   Margherita Guarducci, *The Primacy of the Church of Rome,* 93–101.

214   Zenit Staff, "Papal Address in Czestochowa: 'Place Yourselves in the School of Mary,'" Zenit, May 26, 2006, https://zenit.org/articles/papal-address-in-czestochowa/ (accessed May 4, 2017).

215   "Pope Francis prays at the Black Madonna of Czestochowa," *Rome Reports*, July 28, 2016, http://www.romereports.com/2016/07/28/ pope-francis-prays-at-the-black-madonna-of-czestochowa (accessed May 4, 2017).

216   "Montevergine: Madonna di Montevergine," www.interfaithmary .net/pages/Montevergine.htm (accessed July 21, 2016).

217   Guarducci, *The Primacy of the Church of Rome*, 93–107.

218   Ibid., 101–7.

219   "La profesora Guarducci ha sido un raro ejemplo de constancia, integridad y absoluta dedicación a la búsqueda de la verdad. Os lo repito, la profesora Guarducci habla como creyente, yo no soy creyente. Lo

que no me impide expresarle mi alta admiración y suscribir hasta la última palabra todo lo que ha dicho." Translated: "The professor Guarducci was a rare example of perseverance, integrity and absolute dedication to the pursuit of truth. I repeat, the professor Guarducci speaks as a believer, I'm not a believer. This does not prevent me expressing my high admiration and [I] subscribe to the last word [to] everything you said." In Castellotti, "El lugar del Primado."

220   Zander, *The Necropolis under St. Peter's Basilica in the Vatican*, 29.

221   "Pope: Basilica bones belong to apostle St. Paul," CNN, June 29, 2009, http://www.cnn.com/2009/WORLD/europe/06/29/vatican.st.paul.bones/index.html?_s=PM:WORLD (accessed May 4, 2017).

222   Baglioni, "Peter Is Here."

223   "The Ten Primitive Persecutions," in *Foxe's Book of Martyrs*, http://www.bibleprobe.com/10persecutions.htm (accessed July 18, 2017).

224   Thomas Gray, "Elegy Written in a Country Churchyard," (1751), Thomas Gray Archive. http://www.thomasgray.org/cgi-bin/display.cgi?text=elcc (accessed September 22, 2016).

225   "The Tomb of Paul VI," Vatican Grottoes, St. Peter's Basilica Info, http://stpetersbasilica.info/Grottoes/Paul%20VI/Tomb%20of%20Paul%20VI.htm and https://w2.vatican.va/content/paul-vi/en/speeches/1978/august/documents/hf_p-vi_spe_19780810_testamento-paolo-vi.html (accessed August 2, 2017).

226   Bianchi, "A Life in the Footsteps of Peter."

227   "Via Margherita Guarducci," *Nuove Strade*, March 18, 2015, http://nuove-strade.it/lazio/roma/via-margherita-guarducci/ (May 12, 2017); "Vatican unveils the bones of St. Peter," *New York Post*, November 24, 2013, nypost.com/2013/11/24/vatican-unveils-the-bones-of-st-peter/ (accessed May 12, 2017).

228   "The Exclusive Tour of Necropolis below St. Peter's Basilica," *Travel+Style*, http://www.travelplusstyle.com/magazine/vatican-top-secret-the-exclusive-tour-of-necropolis-below-st-peters-basilica (accessed May 12, 2017).

229   Zander, *The Necropolis under St. Peter's Basilica in the Vatican* (citing Jesus' prophecy in John 21:18 that Peter would die in old age through crucifixion: "When you were young, you girded yourself and walked where you would; but when you are old, you will stretch out your hands, and another will gird you and carry you where you do not wish to go.").

230 Guarducci, Peter, 25–26; Landry, "Hidden Treasure."

231 Guarducci, *The Tomb of St. Peter*, 94.

232 Jareen Imam, "Scientists to drill at site of dinosaur-killing asteroid crater," CNN, March 4, 2016, www.cnn.com/2016/03/04/world/scientists-drill-impact-crater-irpt/index.html (accessed August 2, 2017); NASA released a high-res map showing the 112-mile-wide, 3,000-foot-deep crater, "'Dinosaur-Killer' Asteroid Crater Imaged for First Time," *National Geographic*, March 7, 2003, www.news.nationalgeographic.com/news/2003/03/0307_030307_impactcrater.html (accessed August 2, 2017).

Acknowledgments

Scripture texts in this work are taken from the *New American Bible, revised edition* © 2010, 1991, 1986, 1970 Confraternity of Christian Doctrine, Washington, D.C., and are used by permission of the copyright owner. All rights reserved. No part of the *New American Bible* may be reproduced in any form without permission in writing from the copyright owner.

Photos used in this book are courtesy of the Strake family, the Our Sunday Visitor photo archives, Newscom, and Fabbrica di San Pietro, Vatican.